on track ...
Van der Graaf Generator

every album, every song

Dan Coffey

sonicbondpublishing.com

Sonicbond Publishing Limited
www.sonicbondpublishing.co.uk
Email: info@sonicbondpublishing.co.uk

First Published in the United Kingdom 2020
First Published in the United States 2020

British Library Cataloguing in Publication Data:
A Catalogue record for this book is available from the British Library

Copyright Dan Coffey 2020

ISBN 978-1-78952-031-6

Typeset in ITC Garamond & ITC Avant Garde
Printed and bound in England

Graphic design and typesetting: Full Moon Media

Acknowledgements

Stephen Lambe, thank you for the opportunity to write this book. The music of Van der Graaf Generator has been in my blood since I turned 18. And that's a lot of years to have something coursing through one's veins! What a gift to be able to put words to my appreciation of the enigma that is VdGG, and send them out into the world.

Speaking of gifts, thank you, Ann Coffey, for being the quintessential 'cool aunt' that bought me the *Pawn Hearts* and *Godbluff* CDs for my 18th birthday, irrevocably warping my mind and sending me down this sometimes lonely but always rewarding path. I'd also like to thank everyone who was in a position to guide me along that path; Harry at Heavy Metal Records in Webster, New York, and Andrew at Lakeshore Record Exchange in Rochester, New York: I'm looking at you.

Thank you, Martin Lowe and Janette Kidd of the 'Top of the World Club' for all your enthusiasm over the past few years, and to Lise Kunkel, Emily Smith, Hannah Hannover, Matt O'Neal, and John Armstrong for your unrelenting faith and support.

Thanks to Peter Hammill, Guy Evans, and especially Hugh Banton, for opening the door eleven years ago in Cleveland, and for your generosity over the years.

Most of all, I want to thank you, Genya and Elliott. You gave me such incredible support through this project, and I literally would not have finished the book without it. I dedicate it to you, and look forward to hanging out with the best wife and son I could have ever hoped for, seeing this book on the shelf out of the corner of my eye, and humming along in unison to VdGG on the stereo – well, as to that last bit, I can dream, can't I?

on track ...
Van der Graaf Generator

Contents

Introduction

It's a testament to the exploratory and experimental quality of much of the music industry at the tail end of the 1960s in Britain that a band with the decidedly unwieldy name Van der Graaf Generator could ever get a foothold, much less establish a decades-spanning career. Indeed, the name more than hints at the musical equivalent of electrostatic interference which would characterise the music to come.

Among the legions of bands that came into being in Britain in the late 1960s, Van der Graaf Generator was virtually unparalleled in its single-minded and relentless devotion to bringing the rock idiom to previously unscaled heights and unplumbed depths. When viewed in a historical context, VdGG is often lumped into the 'progressive rock' genre, and while this isn't entirely unfair, it's also not terribly accurate. They did tick some of the standard prog rock hallmark boxes – long songs, knotty time signatures and ambitious lyrics – but they didn't share the pomp and the focus on presenting note-perfect renditions of their recorded works on the stage. This set them apart from contemporaries like Yes, Jethro Tull, and Emerson, Lake and Palmer, for whom a static representation of their oeuvre was paramount, and put them more in the company of bands at the more radical and improvisational end of the spectrum – Faust, Can, and the *Larks' Tongues in Aspic* era King Crimson.

The brainchild of two Manchester University students, Peter Hammill and Chris Judge Smith, VdGG – like many of their contemporaries – had quite a few false starts before taking off in earnest. *The Aerosol Grey Machine*, VdGG's 1969 debut, started off a recording career that was modest in its quantity, but brilliant in intensity. Three more albums were generated before the band's untimely implosion. 1972-1975 saw Hammill, the band's singer and principal songwriter, focusing on a solo career and releasing a clutch of critically acclaimed albums. He was joined by his erstwhile bandmates on many of the tracks on these albums, and although there's no question that the songs on these records bore the stamp of the individual artist rather than the group, there are nevertheless a number of compositions that are thoroughly imbued with the VdGG spirit – and, indeed, these songs would enter the band's repertoire upon their reformation.

And reform they did – in a short, intense burst of activity, the band released one album in 1975 and two in 1976, before imploding once again. 1977 saw Hammill grabbing the reins for one last round, bringing in new musicians to replace those who had left, and removing 'Generator' from the name. A studio album that year and a live album in 1978 bookended VdGG's brilliant and tempestuous decade-long run. The band members created their own musical pathways and continued to collaborate with Hammill to greater and lesser extents through the years, as he went on to build up an impressive body of work.

Of course, the VdGG book, though closed for many years, didn't remain that way. A few tentative reunions in the 1990s indicated to the now-classic four-piece line up (Hugh Banton on organ, Guy Evans on drums, saxophonist and flautist David Jackson, and Peter Hammill on vocals, guitar and keyboards) that future projects as a reformed band weren't out of the question. It wasn't until 2004, however, that such a move seemed completely reasonable or desirable. After a period of low-key rehearsals out of the public eye, the four musicians decided to reform, and VdGG has been a going concern ever since. The story of VdGG is one of attrition: starting as a five-piece outfit, they reconfigured early on in their career to a quartet, which remains their most well-known and loved format. Aside from the brief foray into 'Van der Graaf' in 1977, it was this quartet that recorded the most seminal VdGG albums in the 1970s, and it was this four-piece that reunited in the 21st century, releasing another studio album in 2005. Shortly after the band's return, however, David Jackson left the fold; VdGG, contrary in spirit and as drawn to challenge as ever, continued on as a trio, eager to see what could be accomplished in such a stripped-down format. To date, the 21st century incarnation of the band has released four more studio albums and undertaken a number of exceedingly ambitious – and successful – concert tours.

This book will chronicle, in detail, the band's studio output from 1969-1978 and 2005-2016. We will also take a close look at Peter Hammill's solo albums in the interim between VdGG Mark I and Mark 2, as they are very much part of the Van der Graaf story, as well as a roundup of the highlights of VdGG band member contributions to solo Hammill albums during the extended dormant period. The album 'Over', released in 1977, however, is not included here. Although some of that album's songs feature the playing of Guy Evans and Nic Potter, it is quite distant from Hammill's work up to that point and really doesn't jive with the VdGG canon in the same way that his earlier albums do. A discussion of VdGG-related odds-and-ends recordings will follow, along with a detailed look at the live recordings, of which there are many in the 21st Century incarnation of the band.

The Aerosol Grey Machine (1969)

Personnel:
Hugh Banton: piano, organ, percussion, backing vocals
Keith Ellis: bass, backing vocals
Guy Evans: drums and percussion
Peter Hammill: vocals, acoustic guitar
Jeff Peach: flute
Produced at Trident Studios, July 31 and August 1, 1969 by John Anthony.
US release date and label: September 1969; Mercury. European release date and label: June, 1974; Vertigo.
Running time: 46:13

The Aerosol Grey Machine took a number of years to build, and it was the apparatus that, in turn, was essential in laying the groundwork for the legendary oeuvres of both Van der Graaf Generator and its principal songwriter, the singer/musician Peter Hammill. Although released in 1969, it was the culmination of an intense and compressed period of time that contained an inordinate amount of trials and pitfalls. Most of these artists would soon be ejected from the Generator, but nevertheless were crucial to its formation.

Hammill and Chris Judge Smith, a drummer, met keyboardist Nick Pearne in 1967, and that trio was the first incarnation of Van der Graaf Generator. Hammill had been writing songs prodigiously, while Smith had just returned from a trip to San Francisco and was inspired by what he saw in that city's counterculture scene to form a band and 'write weird music', as he told Jim Christopulos. Smith also is credited with coming up with the band name – it was one among a list of potential candidates that he'd compiled which mixed modern science with the absurd. One contender was 'Zeiss Manifold and the Shrieking Plasma!' For whatever reason (perhaps because Robert J. Van de Graaff, creator of the device that bears his name, died that year, and so was frequently in the news), Van der Graaf Generator was the name that was chosen, and it stuck, misspellings and all.

Before long, Pearne decided to quit VdGG to focus on his studies, and he was replaced by Hugh Banton. Smith also decided to opt out, and Guy Evans entered the fold. Turning the trio into a quartet was bassist Keith Ellis, late of The Koobas, who had a minor hit with their rendition of 'The First Cut Is the Deepest'. Prior to these additions to the roster, Hammill and Smith, too eager to jump into the process of getting a record out, signed a bad contract. When the new foursome went into the studio to cut a single ('People You Were Going To' b/w 'Firebrand') and released it one week later on the Polydor label, Mercury, the contract-holder, issued a cease-and-desist order, and the single was immediately recalled. It had a literal shelf-life of one week.

The upshot of all this being that VdGG, as represented by Hammill's signature, was not allowed to release any music except through Mercury, who had no immediate plans to do anything of the sort. Thus, the band split up, and Hammill, free to record under his own name, decided to record a solo album and called on the other erstwhile VdGG members to help out in the studio. In the course of the three-day recording session that resulted in *The Aerosol Grey Machine*, which was going to be, according to Hammill, a collection of gentle songs, Hammill, Banton, Ellis and Evans realized that it was in fact a 'band' album and that they were, for all intents and purposes, back together.

It wasn't that simple, however, and their new manager, Tony Stratton-Smith, had to perform some complicated record biz gymnastics to get VdGG out of its contract with Mercury. In the end, Mercury agreed to release the record and release the band from the contract. Stratton-Smith was the head of Charisma Records, a label that was mainly started to give VdGG a home and allow them to release records in the future, but of course, it became a much larger concern and a home to musical acts like Genesis and later, Peter Gabriel as a solo artist.

Hammill, in the liner notes to his 1997 version of *Aerosol*, recalls that the album which the four-piece were intent on making before Mercury's legal injunction would have been quite different than what actually emerged after Mercury and Stratton-Smith came to an agreement. He explains that the original concept was more closely tied to songs like 'Octopus' and 'Necromancer' (the 'neo-naff mystical'), and would have included songs like 'White Hammer', which, of course, was eventually placed on the band's second album. Instead, *Aerosol* leaned more towards what Hammill describes as 'neo-love songs'. The album, minus 'Afterwards' and 'Necromancer' which were recorded some months earlier, was recorded in twelve hours and mixed in half that time.

Aerosol was initially only released in the United States, available in the band's home country only as an import. Two versions of *Aerosol* were released in the US in 1969. One was a mis-pressing that substituted the song 'Giant Squid' for 'Necromancer', which was intended for the album and appears on the tracklist on the back cover. This pressing was quickly recalled and replaced with the correct pressing. It was reissued five years later in Italy and the Netherlands, and in Germany in 1975, but wasn't released in the UK until 1997, as a compact disc.

1997 was a pivotal year in the long and strange history of this album. First, Repertoire Records got hold of the original recordings and rights, and re-released the album on CD, including two 'bonus' tracks: 'People You Were Going To' and 'Firebrand', the A and B sides, respectively, of a single that was released just prior to the album in January 1969. Spurred on by what he felt was at best a misrepresentation of the album, Hammill released an alternate version of *Aerosol* on his own FIE! label. In addition to at last remastering the tracks, Hammill included a different pair of 'bonus' tracks: 'Ferret & Featherbird' which had never been commercially released (it was re-recorded for Hammill's 1974 solo album *In Camera*), and 'Giant Squid', the song that briefly appeared on the 1969 mis-pressed version of the LP.

And so, the story of *The Aerosol Grey Machine* was completed – for a time. In 2019, on the 50th anniversary of the album's release, a commemorative box set edition was released, containing two CDs, a vinyl LP, and a 7' record. The first CD is the 1997 FIE! version of the album, and the second CD contains four tracks of BBC sessions that were first aired on 18 November 1968, bookended by two previously unreleased demos, 'Firebrand' and 'Sunshine', and the A and B sides of the band's first single, 'People You Were Going To' backed with 'Firebrand'. The LP has the same tracklist as the original version of the album, and the 7' record is a replica of the original January 1969 single release.

'Afterwards' (Hammill)

It's fair to consider it somewhat perverse to open Side A of a debut album with a song called 'Afterwards', but for VdGG it made sense. Lyrically, at least, it contained the seeds of some of the qualities that would become Hammill's hallmarks in subsequent years: an unwavering gaze into the darker aspects of human nature and existence, and the commitment to remaining unbowed by what might be discovered in that scrutiny. It's a relatively simple pop song with an unusual angle; having described and dispensed with the beauty and preciousness of newly found romantic love, Hammill examines the all-too-common ways in which such encounters fizzle out, with one partner not taking the necessary leap of faith. For the protagonist's counterpart, 'the petals that were blooming are just paper', and what was momentarily vibrant becomes rigid, static, and artificial.

Three beats from Evans's bass drum introduce this song, and then Hugh Banton's wah-wah infused organ kicks in, bringing with it a potent psychedelic haze that swirls around Hammill's gentle acoustic guitar and Ellis's subdued but assertive bass. The playing is more than capable, but what elevates the song from eye level to the rarefied atmosphere it's been enjoying for fifty years is Hammill's vocal performance. Delicate in tone but earthy in substance, the first appearance of Hammill's once-in-a-lifetime voice is at once as pleasurable and discomfiting as one who is familiar with his career output might expect. The tune is certainly vibrant, and Peter's fallen-angelic vocals belie a certain toughness to the music, borne on the strumming of the acoustic guitar and Hugh's double-duty on organ and piano, as well as the unique, almost primitive, sound of Keith Ellis's bass.

'Afterwards', alone among the songs on *Aerosol*, enjoyed a life beyond the album's release and hasty disappearance from the view of the record-buying public; eight years later Hammill would revisit it, his vocals and acoustic guitar accompanied by Graham Smith on violin, for one of John Peel's famous live in-studio sessions to be broadcast on the BBC. This recording was briefly made available on a Peter Hammill 'Peel Sessions' compilation CD in 1995; like *Aerosol*, it didn't remain in print for long. 'Afterwards' also found its way into Hammill's go-to batch of songs that frequently peppered his concert playlists for the remainder of his touring career. It was also released as a single on Mercury in the US, more or less concurrently with *Aerosol*, with 'Necromancer' as its B-side.

'Orthenthian St' (Hammill)

While 'Afterwards' stays at one constant, languorous, speed, the velocity of the next song on the album, 'Orthenthian St', is in flux. It's also in two parts; not by intent, as Hammill again explains in the 1997 liner notes, but due to lack of time and money to edit the recording properly (the two parts were later joined in that 1997 reissue). Infused with a youthful bravado (and self-importance), various scenarios and modes of travelling are put forth in the lyrics; in each, the protagonist declares the need to make a journey alone and temporarily leave his partner behind, but also a sense that he very much wants that partner to remain with him after adventuring (being young is so complicated!). Add in a few early observations of the automobile as a metaphor for both the illusion of the present and the vehicle that carries us into the future that are more successfully fleshed out in later songs like 'Sitting Targets', and some furious piano-pounding from Banton and bass-plucking from Ellis, and you have a fun, rollicking slice of existential rock.

'Running Back' (Hammill)

'Running Back' is a partial return to the fragility of 'Afterwards', as well as a deep dive into what would become known as progressive rock. The third track on *Aerosol* moves with the deliberate pace of one who has made a profound, and perhaps uncomfortable, decision. Hammill's lyrical conceit of 'running back' to the thing in his life that he once thought he longed to be free from is well suited by the slower, more ponderous tempo. The titular phrase is declaimed in an unhurried fashion, but at the same time is filled with a committed bravado seemingly born of hard-won self-awareness that belies the singer's age. It's interesting to note the parallels, lyrically and musically, between 'Running Back' and 'Refugees', the band's first bona fide 'classic', which would appear a year later. In both, Hammill, invokes directional metaphors, naming East and West as signifiers of doom and hopefulness, respectively, and the band cover similar ground – a melancholy merry-go-round of subdued festiveness and upbeat elegy.

Jeff Peach's flute work (the only appearance he makes on the original version of *Aerosol*) intermingles with the threads laid down by the rest of the band, and acoustic guitar, keyboards, percussion (Evans never goes beyond rapping out the beat with a stick on an unidentified dull surface) and bass are lightly galloping across the sonic field with a sprightliness that belies the more dolorous tone of the opening verses. When the band return to the established structure of the song's main theme, we are privy to some full-throated vocals which, as a whole, are delivered in a register lower than we've heard so far from Hammill. He didn't exactly shrink from the mic in the first two songs, but on 'Running Back', there seems to be less of a concern with a pop singer's coy restraint, and more of an attempt to match the sense behind the words with honest, and unaffected emotion, from near-falsetto crooning to throat-abusing heroics.

'Into a Game' (Hammill)

'Into a Game' has more of the prematurely jaded and seemingly emotionally spent musings that informed 'Orthenthian St' and 'Afterwards' – anti-love songs that provide a foil for 'Running Back'. It opens with the by now somewhat familiar approach of strummed acoustic guitar, galloping bass, and piano that, here, is quite restrained, with notes that are as resounding as they are cautious. Evans is last to jump into the pool, with his commanding drum flourishes entering alongside Hammill's vocals. Evans really takes the emergency brake off here, drumming with a frenzied abandon.

While not as inspired as the previous three tracks, 'Into a Game' certainly doesn't reflect poorly on the band. Hammill's lyrics skate closer to cliché and the band play capably, if not exactly with the same inspiration that fuelled the earlier cuts. The song comes to a false end as Hammill's lyrically terse and frustrated explanation of why a troubled relationship is petering (pardon the pun) out. In this second part of the song (the entire band is credited as writing 'Into a Game Part II' while the first part is, as usual, credited solely to Hammill), after a considerable pause, Evans counts the band back in, every bit as much in the forefront as he was in the first part. Ellis and Banton join in formation, with the latter's piano playing much more spirited than the main part of the song. Hammill has set the guitar down, but can be heard down in the mix leading a choral repetition of the title phrase, with Banton and Ellis singing even further in the background. The melding of voices is slightly discordant but very effective – a trademark of VdGG in the years to come, although the vocals would be solely Hammills.

'Aerosol Grey Machine' (Hammill)

Side B of *Aerosol* opens with a bit of light comedy, with the short, campy title track, which sounds more like an ad jingle-cum-show tune than an art-pop song. A healthy sense of humour would always be a central part of VdGG's identity, but in the years to follow would only be publicly visible in the context of live performances. On record, there would only be a very few moments of levity, and these were subtly woven into the compositions. 'Aerosol Grey Machine' (the song), however, came into being in the midst of youthful uncertainty and record industry flux – the band, paradoxically, had to deal with at least as many wrenches being thrown into their carefully balanced works as they did through the seventies, when they had gained considerably more experience. They needed – and were thankfully able to – cut loose a little.

The song was written while Judge Smith was still a member of the band, and the phrase, according to Christopulos and Smart's history of VdGG, can be attributed to Hammill, who jokingly addressed Smith's high sensitivity to psychedelic drugs, which were at the time, Smith says, dropped very liberally into the drinks of unsuspecting bar patrons. Hammill suggested that Smith might need an 'aerosol grey machine' which could counter the effects of LSD and similar consciousness-altering drugs by making everything artificially grey.

Hammill camps it up on the lead vocal, channelling the spirit of Monty Python (who would soon become recording labelmates with VdGG on the yet to be formed Charisma Records), declaiming the outrageous lyrics: 'Well, you're walking along the road one day / Up comes a man dressed all in grey / He blows a little aerosol in your face / And you find your mind's all over the place!' Banton and Ellis provide backing vocals, and Hammill and Banton supply, as well, the two sides to a comic dialogue that closes the song – the former acting as a disembodied advertising voice-over with a delightfully cartoonish delivery, while the latter is a steadfast naysayer who is not buying this nonsense: 'Shan't, shan't. I'm not going to!'

'Black Smoke Yen' (Banton, Ellis, Evans)

'Black Smoke Yen', a titular rejoinder to the previous song, perhaps, is only slightly longer than 'The Aerosol Grey Machine', clocking in at about 90 seconds. It is a Hammill-less instrumental in which Banton, Ellis, and Evans gel as a progressive rock trio. The composition is credited to these three; Hammill is the sole composer of the rest of the songs on *Aerosol*, save for the latter part of 'Into a Game'. It's not as flashy as Yes's 'Five Percent for Nothing' perhaps, but it shows a depth of feeling and musical empathy that is rare in general and even more so among a group of musicians as young as these three.

Evans, once again, introduces the tune, followed shortly by Ellis, and then Banton on piano. Ellis matches Evans's beats with repeated three-note clusters, that, when listened to against Banton's own sympathetic but not quite parallel three-note clusters of his own, create a slightly dissonant effect that would be hypnotising if it were allowed to go on longer. The riffs cease too soon, fading as Hammill's acoustic guitar phases in – part of the introduction to the next track that bleeds backwards into the close of 'Black Smoke Yen'.

'Aquarian' (Hammill)

Along with the album's closing track, 'Octopus', 'Aquarian' is a lengthy track at almost ten minutes. Unlike most songs of similar length in the VdGG canon, 'Aquarian' doesn't consist of a series of ever-changing parts; it chugs along for its entire length in a consistently anthemic vein. Musically and lyrically, 'Aquarian' has more in common with the upbeat feel of many of the songs on Hammill's 1971 solo album, *Fool's Mate* – most of which were written around the same time as this one. With the partial exception of 'Orthenthian Street', 'Aquarian' is the only song on this album to apply a wide-angle approach to the lyrics, replacing the 'I' with 'we', and looking beyond personal experience to capture a snapshot of late 1960s youth culture. There's an unmitigated, at times giddy, joy emanating from 'Aquarian', but it's easy to forgive the band, and particularly Hammill, for veering into silliness, because there is nothing here that seems forced or affected. This would have worked well as the album closer, with lyrics that refer back to 'Afterwards' – albeit in a quite different context – as well as the album title: 'I hold silver flashing metal in the palm / of my petal hand, watching it quiver: / to breathe too close is death – / ah, but what is breath but a way to deliverance? / Soon we will all be joined / in our great silver tube…'

The optimism that runs through the lyrics is infectious. Banton seems to have been most affected by the bug, doing double-duty on piano and organ, the latter far down in the mix at the beginning, but gradually gaining volume and heft as the song progresses, majestically swirling and soaring around and above the drums, bass, and acoustic guitar. All the instruments are recorded brightly and sound as though they are about to burst out of the speakers to join Hammill's eponymous Aquarians, 'writing our names as we move to the sun'. Most of VdGG's music is accurately described as 'life-affirming', the idea being that despite the darkness that characterises much of their recorded output, the fact that such music is being made is inherent proof of its positivity – something that Hammill has said often about his own work. With 'Aquarian', though, there's no need for such proof – this is a rare Van der Graafian moment of pure and unmitigated celebration.

'Necromancer' (Hammill)

After the stirring crescendo of 'Aquarian', 'Necromancer' feels like a bit of a post-credits extra reward for the committed. It is as different as 'Aquarian' from the other songs on *Aerosol*. A concise, radio-friendly length, it is, musically, the most-straightforward rock song on the album, albeit with plenty of strange and spooky organ effects to go along with the very serious silliness of the lyrics that illustrate mysticism and magic in the manner of a late 1960s comic book. It's certainly fun, but probably not one of the VdGG songs a fan would return to very often. Here, again, Banton plays piano and organ, and Ellis's performance on bass is by far the heaviest and most electric sounding of his *Aerosol* contributions.

'Octopus' (Hammill)

In one sense, at least, closing the album with 'Octopus' is fitting: Banton's distinctive organ sound has crossed a divide that separates the sound of the rest of *Aerosol* from future VdGG albums – particularly the two that immediately follow. The band's approach on 'Octopus' is altogether more menacing and aggressive than the previous tracks. Banton foregoes the piano this time, stabbing at chords on his organ to help propel the song, while also using the instrument to generate an atmosphere of tension. Three verses bookend the lengthy instrumental section; Hammill dispenses quickly with the first two and gets out of the way so that Banton and Ellis can face off in a maritime battle royal. Already having established himself on *Aerosol* as a bassist with a distinctive sound, here Ellis cuts loose and displays some wicked chops, resulting in a spellbinding duet performance alongside Banton. Unexpectedly, the two musicians are abruptly becalmed, allowing Banton to change direction and immerse the listener in gentler washes of sound. Before long, Evans comes in on drums and picks the pace back up. The trio sail on once again, eventually bringing Hammill back into the fold to deliver the final verse and refrain, with vocals that are fierier yet than anything he's put forth so far on *Aerosol*. Perhaps not as thematically fitting a closing statement as 'Aquarian' might have been, 'Octopus' nevertheless ends the album with an enormous and resounding bang.

Bonus Tracks on Later Editions
'Ferret & Featherbird' (Hammill)

Rescued from the *Aerosol Grey Machine* recording sessions when Peter Hammill released his specially curated version of the album, the song can be found nestled between 'Into a Game' and the title track. Until 1997, the only commercially released VdGG song that Jeff Peach's flute could be heard on was 'Running Back'.

'Ferret' begins innocuously with gentle strumming and crooning from Hammill, backed with an equally laidback contribution on bass from Ellis. Tempo and energy are kicked up a notch in the second verse when Peach and Evans come in on flute and drums. Banton is last to join in, on piano, during the bridge, which is when the song almost takes off, with the band accelerating and Hammill increasing the volume of his vocal delivery. It doesn't last, and the song quickly settles back on the ground, finishing with relative calm.

A version of this song with a markedly different arrangement can be found on Hammill's 1974 album *In Camera* – for many years, the only commonly known version of this song to exist in recorded format.

'Giant Squid' (Banton, Ellis, Evans, Hammill)

The second song pulled from the *Aerosol* recording session vaults for Hammill's 1997 CD version of the album is a companion to 'Octopus'. One of the shortest songs on the album, it's almost entirely instrumental, save for an introductory couplet sung by Hammill, the lyrics of which sit well with its deep-sea cousin. His vocals are accompanied by what is at this point a standard Evans/Ellis sound, with Banton adding organ, set to approximate a flute-like tone, to the mix. Hammill's acoustic guitar takes centre stage for a sizable portion of the song, with pairs of slashing chords punctuating the silence, eventually accompanied by Ellis on bass. Evans comes back in with a faster, more strident beat, as does Banton, foregoing the flute setting for his standard organ sound. The band's interplay starts to take off but doesn't reach a destination before the track starts to fade out. 'Giant Squid' did make a brief and rare appearance on a mis-pressed version of the original 1969 release, which was quickly recalled. A live performance of this song, interwoven with 'Octopus', can be found as a bonus track on the 2005 remastered re-release of VdGG's 1970 album *H to He Who Am the Only One* – it was recorded for the BBC during the run-up to that album's original release.

'People You Were Going To' (Hammill)
This is from an earlier recording than the sessions that produced the original *Aerosol* album. 'People' sounds a bit rough by comparison – the band seem to be hurrying to get through it. Hammill would revisit it years later for his solo *Nadir's Big Chance* album.

'Firebrand' (Hammill)
Another very early recording, 'Firebrand' appears twice on the 2019 box set edition of *Aerosol* – as a demo recorded in 1967 and as the B-side of the blocked single, recorded in January 1969. It first appeared in digital format as a bonus track on Repertoire Records' 1997 release of *Aerosol*. Hammill sings lead on the demo version sounding a good deal more placid than he would even one year later. Chris Judge Smith supplies rudimentary drums and backing vocals towards the end. The keyboards are a great example of the pre-Hugh Banton era; Nick Pearne acquits himself well.

The official version of 'Firebrand' features the extremely short-lived five-piece line-up of early 1969, when Banton, Ellis, and Evans had joined but before Smith departed. This 'Firebrand' is definitive VdGG, from the swirling, oppressive haze of Banton's organ to the equally atmospheric hail-pelt of Evans's cymbals, and underpinned by Ellis' intricate but rather faint bass riffing. Not for the first time does VdGG sound a bit like early Deep Purple! Smith provides hyper-emotive vocals on the choruses, in the speaker opposite Hammill. Interestingly, his extreme style of singing hints at the approach that Hammill would come to take as VdGG matured and his solo career took off.

The lyric is based on, and faithful to, an Icelandic saga. Cut from the same cloth as 'Necromancer', 'Firebrand' is more successful, in part because the focus of the song is cast on the telling of the story, while in 'Necromancer' more attention is given to extraneous moralising.

'Sunshine' (Hammill)
The second of two demos unearthed from the 1967 line up of Hammill/Pearne/Smith, 'Sunshine' is a simple tune that is unabashedly silly and awash in unrestrained glee. After a somewhat lengthy intro that sounds like it's being played on a calliope, the men who would be VdGG turn in an energetic bare-bones performance on acoustic guitar, keyboards, and drums. Hammill's vocals aren't too different from the later version of the song that would find its way on to his first solo album, *Fool's Mate*. Here, as on the demo of 'Firebrand', Smith provides backing vocals, but unlike the other demo, he doesn't play it straight; zany vocal extemporisations are inserted in the breaks between verses

and chorus, and during the instrumental section, Smith goes full-tilt whacko, madly scatting and gibbering.

BBC Live in Studio Tracks

These tracks were first broadcast on the BBC programme Top Gear Sessions on 18 November 1968.

'People You Were Going To' (Hammill)
'Afterwards' (Hammill)
'Necromancer' (Hammill)
'Octopus' (Hammill)

Of these four selections, 'People' is closest to the studio version, but this recording suffers from audio dropouts frequently in the beginning and more sporadically as the performance continues. 'Afterwards' features a rougher, more intense vocal delivery from Hammill, but a looser approach from the rest of the band – the baroque instrumental middle section is absent from this performance. 'Necromancer' is played with a ferociousness that speaks to the live energy for which the band would come to be known. These three recordings also appear on the compilation of BBC performances, *After the Flood*, which was released in 2015. 'Octopus', however, is absent from that collection and only appears here, in the *Aerosol* box set. The last of these four pushes the needle into the red: the bass end of Banton's organ output is gloriously distorted and at times hard to distinguish from Ellis's bass guitar, and Evans's drums are equally phased. Hammill's delivery is more extreme than the album version, but nowhere near as incandescent as the re-recording to come in 1971.

The Least We Can Do Is Wave to Each Other (1970)

Personnel:

Hugh Banton: organ, piano, backing vocals

Guy Evans: drums, percussion

Peter Hammill: lead vocals, acoustic guitar

David Jackson: alto and tenor saxophones, flute, backing vocals

Nic Potter: bass guitar, electric guitar

Additional musicians:

Mike Hurwitz: cello

Gerry Salisbury: cornet

Produced at Trident Studios, December 1969, by John Anthony.

UK release date and label: February 1970; Charisma. US release date and label: 1970, Probe.

Highest chart place: UK: 47.

In February of 1970, VdGG released *The Least We Can Do Is Wave to Each Other*, the second album credited to the band, but to the way of thinking of many fans, not to mention Peter Hammill, their first real release. It's a markedly different affair from *Aerosol*, with Hammill and Evans both remarking in the immediate aftermath that it was less schizophrenic – *Aerosol* bounced back and forth between psych-pop gems and 'iridescent monsters' (Evans) of songs, whereas *The Least We Can Do* has a more singular focus. The band may have been more focused, but to this writer, their second album still seems to carry with it the tendency to veer towards extremes: check out the serious aural onslaught that lies in waiting in the coda to 'White Hammer', and the unapologetic deep-end of noise in 'Darkness', and compare it to the gentle, sober, 'Refugees' and 'Out of My Book'. VdGG still makes room for both types of music here. While the sweet songs may not be quite as sugary, the intensity of the more manic ones do belie a more focused attention to musical complexity.

According to David Jackson, the album was recorded in four days, although the material was heavily rehearsed in the weeks and months leading up to the studio dates. Interestingly, an early mix of this album squeaked out without the band's blessing or that of engineer John Anthony. When the album was finished, Charisma label boss Tony Stratton-Smith listened, and didn't like how the surface of the record sounded, so, without informing the band, he brought in Shel Talmy, the well-known producer of many singles for popular contemporary recording artists like The Who and The Kinks, to remix the record. While a capable technician, the band felt Talmy's approach was wrong for their music – he was giving a profoundly 'stereo' band a 'mono' mix. Luckily, Talmy's mix of the album was pulled days after it was released, but it's still possible to hear this version; it pops up occasionally on the Internet as a bootleg.

The Least We Can Do was released as a gatefold album, with contemporary photographs of the band members juxtaposed with portraits of them as small children. Many initial copies came with a poster as well. The album was dedicated 'to L. and M., without whom everyone would have been much happier'. The initials referred to Lou Reizner and Mercury Records, who were, of course, responsible for the contract that hobbled the original VdGG line-up. A well-placed quote also on the album's back cover raised the pithiness factor and provided the album's title: 'We are all awash in a sea of blood and the least we can do is wave to each other'. Some editions of this album were listed in the Discogs database with the *Paradise Lost* poet John Milton credited for the quote, but in fact, the words belong to the middle-20th Century British book illustrator John Minton.

Between the release of *Aerosol* and the recording of *The Least We Can Do*, the band waved goodbye to Keith Ellis. Ellis would go on to help form the band Juicy Lucy, which arose from the ashes of The Misunderstood, of which Evans and Potter were members prior to joining VdGG. After two albums with his new band, Ellis moved on to be a part of Boxer, again for two albums. In 1978, he passed away prematurely. Hammill eulogised him in the song 'Not for Keith', which appeared on the solo album *pH7* in 1979. At the same time, 'hellos' were waved to saxophonist David Jackson and bassist Nic Potter, both of whom would be mainstays in the VdGG/Hammill musical world for many years, even though Potter would leave the active band roster shortly. Banton, Evans, and Hammill remained, cementing the core of what, minus Potter, would become the 'classic line-up'.

Potter and Evans, having already played together, were a formidable and well-established rhythm section. Potter also gave Banton a break, freeing him from his bass duties on the organ and allowing him to further shape the Generator's unique sound. Jackson, with his Roland Kirk-inspired 'double sax' attack – blowing through two horns at once – as well as his penchant for electrifying the sonic output of his instruments, provided something akin to what would be the role of a lead guitarist in a more conventional rock band.

'Darkness (11/11)' (Hammill)

The album opens with a breathtaking and uncompromising statement of one's relationship to fate and the creative process. The song enters the sonic threshold on an ominous breath, courtesy of Jackson's playing and the band's sotto voce humming. An insistent, almost martial, beat kicks in, which soon gives way, accompanied by the band, to a thunderous progression. The instrumentation is not quite given over to cacophony until the end nears, and Hammill lets loose with the final, thrice-repeated line of the lyric: 'I did not choose it!'. At this point, Jackson engages in brutal, saxophone-driven noise. Years later, in 1976, Hammill answered fan questions that were sent to a newspaper. Someone asked what the parenthetical '11/11' in the title was referring to. Hammill, in an entirely understandable 'we're in 1976 and there are other songs I'd rather be discussing' mode, informed the fan that he was no longer as interested in numerology as he was in 1969 and that he didn't think about it much. 11/11 is, of course, Remembrance Day in the Commonwealth, and celebrated as Veterans' Day in the US. It also generally figures into numerology as a number containing powerful energy and likely to indicate the potential for radically new beginnings (especially when four 1s are side by side). Many spiritual numerologists claim that 11 November, or indeed the AM or PM occurrence of 11:11, is a period of time rife with the potential for change and growth. 'Darkness' was a staple of VdGG concerts through 1976 and again after the 2005 reunion, and Hammill occasionally played the song in solo performances.

'Refugees' (Hammill, Jackson)
'Darkness' carries a certain amount of weight, regarding legacy, but not nearly as much as the track that follows it. 'Refugees' is VdGG's signature short-form song and is the most widely-anthologised song that the band has recorded and was a staple of VdGG and Hammill concerts, especially in the 21st Century. A gently hypnotic melody with flute from Jackson, and transcendent organ tones from Banton, 'Refugees' is accompanied by Hammill's clear-eyed but melancholic lyrics and stunning vocals that manage to sound youthful and world-weary all at once. Two figures who would appear in future Hammill song lyrics ('Easy to Slip Away', on his 1973 album *Chameleon in the Shadow of the Night*), Mike and Susie, make their first appearance in 'Refugees'. In more recent years, these two characters have been identified as former flatmates of Hammill's: 'Mike' is Mike McLean, and 'Susie' is Susan Penhaligon, a television and film actress. McLean wasn't the only 'Mike' to figure into 'Refugees': guest cellist Mike Hurvitz, a member of the London-based Philharmonia Orchestra and Keith Tippett's jazz/rock outfit Centipede, who performed on the latter's essential *September Energy* album as well as Mott the Hoople's *The Hoople*, and Elton John's *Blue Moves*, also turns in a very moving performance.

'White Hammer' (Hammill)
'Monstrous organ music', Hugh Banton has said about his keyboard contributions to VdGG circa 1969, akin to 'a lot of French church organ music', and that somewhat tongue-in-cheek description is most apt here. In addition to the band, another guest musician appears here: the cornetist/trumpeter Gerry Salisbury, who had already been a session musician for over ten years and was contemporaneously working with Graham Bond on his infamous departure from mainstream blues, the white magic-infused, ritualistic *Holy Magick* album. No surprise that he played on the one VdGG song dealing with white magic!

The bulk of the song is an extended narrative from Hammill, dealing with the Inquisition and the fear of and desire to contain magic at any cost, including torture and other acts that would go against the religious faith they seemed to embrace, in the 15th Century. Hammill sings and writes of a 'white hammer' imbued with the force of retributive white magic, which would, ironically, spell doom for both practitioners of black magic and those whose 'holy' calling was to destroy magic in any form. The band chose to portray the power of the white hammer musically, in a delightfully pulverising coda that more than makes up for the somewhat lugubrious lyrical chronicling and passive instrumental pace-keeping. It is in the closing of the song that the energy of the album is restored to the heights of 'Darkness', closing out Side One.

'Whatever Would Robert Have Said?' (Hammill)
Side Two opens with somewhat of a rarity in the VdGG oeuvre – a song with lead electric guitar. Courtesy of bassist Nic Potter, this was, according to the man himself, the first time he'd attempted playing that instrument! There was a six-string electric guitar in the studio, Potter remembers, and the rest of the band were eager for him to try it. Despite his misgivings, he did, and laid down the tracks that would turn the song – an homage, to an extent, to the inventor of the eponymous machine, Robert J. Van de Graaff – into a vibrant, over-driven prog rock tour de force. The song wasn't performed live very often, but it was immortalised in a performance by the band on the German 'Beat Club' television program, with the five-piece incarnation of VdGG squeezed onto a very small stage and Hammill looking like a Gothic wraith. It's a study in contradictions, both lyrically, and in the very essence of the song itself – a comparatively brief number, it nonetheless contains enough starts, stops, and tempo changes to fuel a full-length prog epic.

'Out of My Book' (Hammill)
This song is a nod back to the pastoral elements of 'Refugees', but it is altogether a more upbeat and poppier affair. Lyrical concerns with the effect of time and ageing on a romantic relationship mines territory similar to the previous album's 'Afterwards', but the focus is less epiphanic and more longitudinal; rather than analysing a certain point in time, Hammill's lyrics are concerned with a wide expanse of time, looking to the overall cumulative effect of past events to try to get a sense of what the future might hold. This song, perhaps more than most Van der Graaf tunes, flirts with what would become FM lite rock of the Southern California variety. Standard conventions of verse and chorus are played with here, with a riff seemingly meant to lead into the latter played, disconcertingly, over and over, long past the usual four repetitions. 'Out of My Book' was played a fair amount by Hammill in solo concerts throughout his career.

'After the Flood' (Hammill)
Despite being placed at the end of side two, this is the album's centrepiece. A scientific rather than occult approach to the terror of humanity meeting its end due to climate change – a prophetic warning, sadly timelicr now

than in 1969 – concealed within over 10 minutes of shapeshifting musical structures that refuse to be pinned down. The song goes back and forth between Hammill's plaintively picked acoustic guitar and the full-on attack of the band, at once lumbering, chugging and soaring. The song contains a middle section that features Hammill half-singing, half-reciting a relevant quote from Albert Einstein. He finishes with the word 'annihilation', which is sung terrifyingly enough, but made still more unsettling by the electronic manipulation to which his vocals are subjected. It's an exhilaratingly intense moment of sonic shock that needs to be experienced to be believed.

'Boat of Millions of Years' (Hammill)

B-Side to 'Refugees' single, released April 17, 1970.

This is a peculiar left-of-centre song that at first resembles a sonic cheat sheet for Egyptian Mythology 101, with no less than four gods name-checked in the first three lines of the song. The lyrics, toward the end, veer from a narrative format that is actually a sort of parable, and become an exhortation to the listener to not give in to their fears, and trust in the goodness of whatever higher powers might exist. In its hewing to the parable form, 'Boat of Millions of Years' shares a kinship with 'White Hammer', and is similarly ungainly, but benefits from an absorbing melody and fascinating experimentation mixed with stellar musicianship—there is an exotic and atmospheric tinge to Jackson's playing, which sees him opting to hold and stretch notes rather than engage in his usual rapid-fire blowing, and Banton echoes this approach on keyboards, while Evans's drumming is perhaps more intense and dynamic than usual, as it comes to the foreground of the musical scenario. It all feels very much like an approximation of what the shifting sands of Egypt might feel like, quickly covering up what was visible and revealing new sights, without resorting to pastiche. On its initial appearance as a B-side, the song was titled 'The Boat of a Million Years'. It was included on a VdGG compilation a year later, *68-71*, where it was re-titled 'The Boat of Millions of Years', and it subsequently lost the 'The'.

'Refugees' (Single version) (Hammill, Jackson)

The 2005 remastered release of the album (the definitive standard for the purposes of this book, as is the case of all the 2005 VdGG reissues, and the solo Hammill reissues from 2005-07) also contains the 'single' version of 'Refugees', released on 24 April 1970. –This recording is a minute shorter than its album-bound counterpart, features a gentler introduction as well as an overall lighter touch from Banton, and, towards the end, pushes Hammill's vocals out further to the front. Yet another recording of this track appears on the budget-priced VdGG compilation, released by the Charisma label in 1980, *Repeat Performance*. It's a remix of the original single version that attempts to make the recording closer in spirit to the album version; the vocals are brought back a little, and the instruments are brought closer to the fore. In 2001, Hammill recorded still another version, live in the studio with just vocals and keyboards, for the soundtrack of the Spanish film *Nos Hacemos Falta*, directed by Juanjo Giménez Peña and released theatrically in 2003.

H to He Who Am the Only One (1970)

Personnel:
Hugh Banton: Farfisa and Hammond organs, oscillator, piano, bass guitar, vocals
Guy Evans: drums, timpani, percussion
Robert Fripp: guitar
Peter Hammill: lead vocals, acoustic guitar
David Jackson: alto, baritone, tenor saxophones, flute, vocals, effects
Nic Potter: bass guitar
Produced at Trident Studios, 1970, by John Anthony.
UK release date and label: December 1970; Charisma. US release date and label:
December 1970: Dunhill
Running time: 46:51

VdGG's third album, released at the close of 1970, *H to He Who Am the Only One* is where the band started to settle into the 'classic' four-piece iteration, with bassist Nic Potter fading out like the protagonist in the album's final song, 'Pioneers Over c'. Potter only played on three of the five tracks that comprised the album. A replacement for Potter was never seriously auditioned, and Banton, feeling the need to close ranks, opted to take on the bass role. He played bass guitar on the two tracks yet to be recorded following Potter's departure: 'House with No Door' and 'Pioneers Over c', and on subsequent live dates would use the organ's pedals to cover the bass. King Crimson guitarist and bandleader Robert Fripp was persuaded by VdGG's producer, John Anthony, to lend his talents to one of the album's tracks. Unlike the recording of the previous year's album, done in four days, *H to He* took many months of sporadic studio dates that were squeezed in among touring obligations.

A decidedly more mature and complex work than *The Least We Can Do*, critics and the public found it more difficult to swallow – it didn't garner the near-universal acclaim that reviews afforded to the previous album. The band, however, was tremendously happy with the way it turned out.

The first half of the album title is a reference to the chemical reaction that occurred at the time of the Big Bang and is also the source of the nuclear reaction that powers the sun. The second part of the title is more mysterious, but the 'H to He' portion can be read vertically as well, like it might appear on the spine of an encyclopaedia volume. Thus, *H to He Who Am the Only One* would theoretically catch-all entries in an imaginary portion of an encyclopaedia that fell into its pages by dint of the alphabet. That range of entries would also, of course, include Hammill.

The evocative artwork that graced the album's cover was painted by the artist Paul Whitehead, who was also responsible for the cover of Hammill's first solo album *Fool's Mate*, and a number of Genesis album covers. Whitehead also illustrated the inner gatefold spread of the LP, over which the lyrics were presented.

'Killer' (Banton, Hammill, Smith)

The album's lead-off track is the other song, besides 'Refugees', that won the band an early following. As a counterpart to the beautifully melancholic earlier song, 'Killer' is a loud, bombastic rocker that serves a purpose similar to 'Darkness' on the previous album – it's a sonic assault that sets the tone, with Jackson blaring and swinging in the foreground. It is punchier and poppier than its elder cousin, and the eight-odd minutes of progressive-meets-anthemic groove consists of three parts that snake around each other: the skeleton of the whole thing, written by Hammill; a more technically demanding part that Banton was responsible for; and a third section that was lifted from a song written by original VdGG member Chris Judge Smith for his post-Generator band Heebalob, 'A Cloud as Big as a Man's Hand'. David Jackson, who had also been in Heebalob, brought this song snippet with him to VdGG to be used in what passes for the 'middle eight' section of the song. Heebalob never got any further than a demo tape, but 'Cloud' (as of this writing) can be heard on YouTube.

'House with No Door' (Hammill, Jackson)

After 'Refugees' was released as a single in the previous year, label heads at Charisma hoped that the band might craft another tune with similarly fragile beauty. That was not to be. The only song on *H to He* that kept the album from being completely shot through with chaotic and wildly temperamental mood shifts was 'House with No Door', but unlike 'Refugees' its particular brand of melancholy was more neurotic than anything that could be considered peaceful. The song's protagonist is not in a healthy frame of mind, and the insistent melodies and rhythms that were picked out by Hammill on piano and Banton on bass pedals bordered on claustrophobic; at best they were uncomfortably insular, giving musical support to the lyrical preponderance of closed doors and windows, and menacing walls which owed more to Edgar Allan Poe than the Walt Whitman-esque sentiments of 'Refugees'.

'The Emperor in His War-Room' (Hammill)

Enter Robert Fripp. When the dust clears, the guest musician hailing from the Court of the Crimson King really deserves the prize of the day. His guitar solos are as biting and sinister as anything he'd done for his own band. Double-tracked, he recorded two solos that run side-by-side with each other in what sounds like an utterly demonic conversation, completely in keeping with the lyrical tone of the piece. What comes before and after the maelstrom of the middle section (which contains some incredible playing from the band as well) never quite seems to fit with the pointedly grotesque lyrical narrative. Jackson's flute gives the song an oddly pastoral feel, and Banton's organ feels like a becalming agent.

This song was rarely played live by the band. Evans confessed later that while he didn't hate it, it felt like a space that he was uncomfortable inhabiting for the length of time it took to perform it. Hammill, looking back, has also expressed a sense of unease regarding the lyrics. Nevertheless, in 1974, Hammill played the song alongside two pieces from his *In Camera* album for a BBC Session.

'Lost' (Hammill)

Following on the heels of the preceding two-part song, 'Lost' is also divided into two subtitled sections. Both Hammill, vocally, and the band, instrumentally, take off from the opening bar with a deliriously winding and twisting procession that at first sounds manically happy. The listener soon realises, however, as VdGG careens in unison around self-manufactured corners and pivot unexpectedly and at curious angles, that, as is often the case with emotions experienced in the extreme, joy is easy to mistake for sorrow. Jackson's sax and Banton's organ are mainly responsible for the confusion; they sound positively bubbly! Hammill eventually provides a more accurate barometer, with a delivery as emphatic as it is morose. And full of self-correcting auto-reprisals ('So here we are, or rather, here am I...').

Eleven minutes later, we're no closer to any sort of resolution, which is just fine – nobody in the throes of love that's become unrequited really wants things to be resolved – but, nevertheless, after many twists and sudden stop/starts, we've arrived at the three-word statement to end all statements, all in caps. Finally, everything gels gloriously – the band abandon themselves to glorious riffage, Hammill puts the apologia down and just tells it straight, and... of course, VdGG couldn't end a song like that! It closes out with a hopscotch between two chords, alternating ever faster as the music begins to fade out. We never hear the final note. It's lost.

'Pioneers Over c' (Hammill, Jackson)

The final track on *H to He* makes it much harder to argue that VdGG was not a progressive rock band, for they've committed one of prog's cardinal sins: writing and recording a bona fide sci-fi epic. Over the sprawling 12 minute track, Hammill tells the story of astronauts who 'left the Earth in 1983' (this is 1970), and, as a result of surpassing the speed of light, found themselves doomed to a ghost-like existence in a 'vacant time-zone', semi-present in all points in time, but fully inhabiting none: 'I am the one who crossed through space / Or stayed where I was / Or didn't exist in the first place...'. The lower-case 'c' in the title is not a typo; it is the symbol that represents the speed of light.

Hammill provided the text for this eerie tale, but the rest of the band really gave it a sensory heft. Banton's organ effects as the song fades in, and during an instrumental break, give the listener a visceral sense of the cold vastness of space. Jackson takes a different tack – his sax solo brings the focus of the song from the distant depths of space to the other extreme: a claustrophobic echo chamber. His playing is so close-miked that his breathing becomes not only noticeable but impossible to ignore. The atonal bleats are disorienting enough, but after some blowing, it gets even weirder. The listener will notice that the sax squeals and honks don't sound quite right, and in fact, Jackson's solo has begun to be rendered backwards. The representation of the arbitrary veil of (what we think of as) time is lifted, and we can hear an approximation of the terror these hypothetical astronauts might have felt. In all, a long and complex work with many components, similar in structure to 'After the Flood' but much more fluid and dynamic, showing how much VdGG had grown in a year's time.

Bonus Tracks
'Squid 1 / Squid 2 / Octopus' (Hammill)

This is a re-recording of 'Giant Squid' and 'Octopus' that was intended for the 1971 *Pawn Hearts* album but was shelved when the Charisma label decided that they wanted to release the album as one LP rather than two, which was the band's intent. It was likely added to the *H to He* 2005 reissue because of the lack of other available recordings relevant to that specific period to use as bonus material and the comparative wealth of recordings already slated for the *Pawn Hearts* reissue. It's not an overstatement to say that this is the most important 'bonus' recording to be unearthed for inclusion on the 2005 remastered VdGG CDs.

This piece had been a consistent staple of VdGG concerts for a few years, and as it had morphed into something different than the studio version present on *Aerosol*, the band decided it would be worthwhile to document the updated version, so they recorded a performance of it at Trident Studios in July 1970. A monolithic 15-minute slab of mostly thunderous and propulsive rock that showcased Evans, Banton, and Jackson in particular as superb improvisers with a connection that seemed to verge on the telepathic.

It begins, as it does on the original version of 'Giant Squid', driven mainly by Hammill's vocals and forceful acoustic guitar strumming. On the 1970 rendition, however, Jackson's sax trills replace Banton's lead organ part, freeing him up to provide washes of colour with the keyboard and to maintain the bass presence that Keith Ellis had originally provided. After the introduction, Hammill bows out rather quickly, leaving the other three to carry on with the mayhem. The riffing on the basic theme of 'Giant Squid' extends for roughly twice the length of the original song, which may account for the 'Squid 1' and 'Squid 2' parts of the title. At about the six-minute mark, VdGG segues into 'Octopus', bringing Hammill back into the fold with a far more unhinged vocal performance than the version recorded two years prior. VdGG soars through the quarter-hour with a vibe of freneticism and euphoria, paving the way for future blissfully complex offerings like the following year's 'Theme One' – it's a side of the band all too often overlooked in favour of some of the darker epic-length tracks.

Fool's Mate (1971)

Personnel:
Hugh Banton: organ, piano
Rod Clements: bass, violin
Guy Evans: drums, percussion
Robert Fripp: electric guitar
Peter Hammill: lead vocals, acoustic guitar, piano
David Jackson: alto and tenor saxophones, flute
Ray Jackson: harp, mandolin
Nic Potter: bass
Martin Pottinger: drums
Paul Whitehead: tam-tam
Produced at Trident Studios, April 1971, by John Anthony.
UK release date and label: July 1971; Charisma. US release date and label: 1972; Charisma.
Running time: 44:28

In the run-up to the recording and release of Van der Graaf Generator's *Pawn Hearts* album, Peter Hammill decided to take a few days of downtime to record some of his older songs for posterity. He was afraid that if he waited any longer to commit them to tape and make them commercially available, too much time would pass between them and the musician he'd become for him to fully inhabit the songs. So, in April 1971, he gathered John Anthony and a cadre of musicians with ties to the Charisma label, including his VdGG bandmates, and in four days recorded the twelve songs that would be released as the album *Fool's Mate* two months later.

All of the songs on *Fool's Mate* date back to Hammill's university days and several were co-written with Judge Smith. Both the album's title and the cover art, once again provided by Paul Whitehead, indicate a conscious nod to the still-forthcoming Van der Graaf release, *Pawn Hearts*, with references to chess. Of the two, Hammill's solo album is more directly allusive. *Fool's Mate* refers to an opening strategy in chess that results in checkmate in only two moves.

'Imperial Zeppelin' (Hammill, Smith)

One of a number of songs in Hammill's catalogue co-written by Judge Smith, this was the first one to appear on a non-VdGG album. 'Imperial Zeppelin' is a concise tour-de-force of a pop song. All members of Van der Graaf Generator, including Nic Potter, perform on this track, as well as Robert Fripp. Martin Pottinger, an associate of Judge Smith, joins Guy Evans on drums. Pottinger played in Heebalob and a few other bands with Max Hutchinson, a frequent collaborator with Smith, and was a roadie for VdGG for a time.

A distinctly Frippian guitar feedback tone introduces the track, providing ten seconds of harsh, disorienting sonics; casual listeners would be forgiven for hitting 'stop' on the remote or quickly lifting the tonearm off of the record. For those who make it through, that stretch of noise can be seen as a threshold that's been crossed which separates the everyday world from the musical dimension which houses the *Fool's Mate* album.

Fool's Mate is not the most otherworldly of records, but it does seem to exist in its own universe, which, whether raucously upbeat or profoundly sombre, is never anything but vibrant and colourful, and, on the other side of Fripp's ambivalent greeting, 'Imperial Zeppelin' is a glorious place for a pair of ears to touch down. The instrumentation is as wide-ranging as it ever gets in the VdGG/Hammill world, with two drummers (as noted above), electric and acoustic guitar (Fripp and Hammill, respectively), bass, and Hugh Banton on piano and organ. All parts of this dirigible are working furiously – Evans is pounding the skins into overdrive, while Pottinger's drumming skitters around the fringes of the soundscape; Banton's organ, after the bridge, throws off incisive trills like electrical sparks, and Fripp's guitar work, as usual, defies logic and description. It all sounds like a recipe for a utopia, and it doesn't last long enough. Though the instruments finally go quiet, the song isn't quite over – the so-called 'Fluctuating Chorale' takes over, hamming it up with an overzealously loony take on the title phrase, while a few voices interject with, 'It's so imperial…'. Shades of *Aerosol*, indeed!

The lyrics are reminiscent of 'Aquarian', from *The Aerosol Grey Machine*, but here the seeds of positivity's demise are embedded within, in the song's bridge: 'Of course, we all know very well, / it wouldn't work, but what the hell'. Still, the song exudes an overwhelming sense of optimism, as Smith's lyrics conjure fantastical images of zeppelins leaving the earth for parts unknown.

'Candle' (Hammill)

Leaving the pen of Judge Smith behind, we're back to solo Hammill compositions, and 'Candle' stands in stark contrast to the previous song. The lyrics are sombre and employ scientific metaphors and a healthy dollop of metaphysics as tools for examining such uncomplicated subjects as spiritual malaise, self-sabotage, and the eventual return of hope to a soul that suffers from these afflictions. 'Candle' has one foot in the VdGG realm of elegiac balladry *a la* 'Refugees' and 'House with No Door', and the other in future Hammill wistfulness that would be at home on *Chameleon in the Shadow of the Night* or *The Silent Corner and the Empty Stage*.

In quite a departure for Hammill, there is no VdGG representation among the other musicians accompanying him. Pottinger, not Evans, is on drums, and, from Charisma labelmates Lindisfarne, Rod Clements and Ray Jackson (no relation to David) join in on the session. Clements plays bass and Jackson is responsible for the hauntingly resonant and stark mandolin that drifts in and out of the recording. Hammill plays guitar throughout, as well as piano, which comes in halfway through the second and third verses.

'Happy' (Hammill)

Thoughtfully, Hammill placed this delightfully oddball nugget of a love song directly after 'Candle' – perhaps mindful of the melancholy mood that the previous song may have cast upon listeners. 'Happy' marks the return of the VdGG team – Nic Potter on bass, David Jackson playing flute and Hugh Banton and Guy Evans on organ and drums, along with Hammill on piano. Although decidedly off-kilter, the sound is nevertheless worlds away from what one would have come to expect from Van der Graaf. Jackson's flute trills dance around the core of the song – Hammill, Banton and Potter playing a repeated four-note riff completely in sync – that is perky and cheerful almost to a fault. Even when it seems like Hammill might have found some shred of darkness that might sink this love boat, it turns out to be only momentary. The darkness quickly disperses, and the band, such as it is, play on, bliss regained.

'Solitude' (Hammill)

The first and final verses of 'Solitude', as Peter Hammill has stated in a compilation CD's liner notes, were 'loosely taken from a poem by Hermann Allmers', with the two middle verses added by Hammill. Allmers was a 19th Century German poet, but 'Solitude' sounds like a cross between British Lake District Romanticism and (thanks to Hammill's lyrical interjection) American Transcendentalism.

The same line-up featured on 'Candle' returns, though this time Hammill plays an effects-enhanced acoustic guitar out in front as opposed to the background embellishments of his strumming on 'Candle'. Ray Jackson trades the mandolin for harmonica, from which he coaxes sounds that are pastoral and psychedelic at the same time while eschewing many of the blues clichés that have come to be associated with the instrument.

'Vision' (Hammill)

'Vision', along with 'The Birds', is one of the two 'classics' featured on *Fool's Mate*. The only instrumentation in the song is Hugh Banton's piano; Hammill sets down the guitar, leaves the keyboard alone, and just sings. The result is a beautiful performance of a profoundly intimate, powerful, song. 'Vision' was briefly performed at VdGG concerts on the tour directly following the release of *Fool's Mate*, and became one of the most frequently performed songs at Peter Hammill concerts throughout the years. It was re-recorded for the 1984 album of revisited solo material, *The Love Songs*, and appeared on an earlier introductory compilation, itself titled *Vision*.

'Re-Awakening' (Hammill)

The five-piece line-up of VdGG, including Nic Potter on bass, are present for this song which skirts the edges of what might be a classic Van der Graaf song. Hammill bashes out the melody on piano while the rest of the musicians ride along in their familiar roles (organ, sax, drums, and bass). Hammill's lyrical concern here is the dichotomy of action and downtime. The narrator defends his proclivity for living in a metaphorical dream-state, telling the listener 'Let me sleep, let me dream, let me be!' There's a similarity to the need to guard one's own path from unwanted encroachment that is evidenced in 'Orthenthian St', which was written around the same time but released several years before on the *Aerosol Grey Machine* album. So, the virtues of dreaming through a life are extolled, but what's really going on here – hence the title – is the apparent difficulty of needing to re-enter the waking world despite being content to be otherwise. The band tear through two verses and two choruses in just over half the song's running time, and the remainder is an exuberant jam over which a choir of voices intone the title and Hammill gives his voice a workout repeating the line, 'Re-awakening isn't easy when you're tired'. It's an excellent song that nicely bridges Hammill's and VdGG's past and present.

'Sunshine' (Hammill)

Side Two of *Fool's Mate* opens with this slice of hyper-joyful pop from Hammill, Banton, Evans, Jackson, Potter, and Robert Fripp. It's simply a delirious love song, and apart from a shot of adrenaline, and uncharacteristically loopy guitar work from Fripp, it sounds very similar to 'Re-Awakening'. Hammill leads the way on vocals and piano, and the rest of the band gallops along gamely in his wake. In the entirety of the VdGG catalogue thus far, there's nothing that matches this level of ecstatic abandon. 'Aquarian' comes close, but even then, there's an acknowledgement that happiness comes at a cost; such concerns don't apply here. 'Sunshine' is the only song from this album for which an early demo recording exists, going back all the way to 1967.

'Child' (Hammill)

'Child' is much more sombre than the previous track. The rest of the musicians remain, save Evans, who sits this one out, but the instrumentation differs. Jackson trades the sax for a flute, Banton ditches the organ for a piano, freeing Hammill to pick up an acoustic guitar. Fripp stays on as well, with a more characteristic pointillist approach, tastefully mimicking the blinking of stars in the nightscape described in the mournful lyrics. Hammill sings of feeling childlike in a state of fear and loneliness. There are some similarities in theme to 'Vision', but where that scenario is mostly a hopeful one wherein the narrator is moving towards a saving grace, there is no such hope evident in this instance. Harsh stabs at the piano keys and a forceful flourish from Jackson's flute reinforce the mood and tone of the lyrics with their almost violent suddenness.

'Summer Song (In the Autumn)' (Hammill)

Another fairly sombre tune, lyrically, 'Summer Song' recoups some of the musical energy of previous tracks. Hammill is back on piano, and what's now become the core group of musicians is back on their usual instruments, but Fripp and Evans sit this one out. Listeners familiar with *The Aerosol Grey Machine* will by now see a lyrical kinship between its songs and the ones on *Fool's Mate*. 'Summer Song' deals in the same sand/sea metaphors as 'Orthenthian St' (and, for that matter, the more recent 'Lost'). The band, such as it is, do a remarkable job at presenting a tasteful pop performance that occasionally verges on an aching beauty, but never loses the kind of street-smart turn of the decade psychedelic rock sound that they seem to be aiming for.

'Viking' (Hammill, Smith)
One of a handful of songs from the early days co-written by Peter Hammill and Chris Judge Smith, 'Viking' indulges heavily in Norse mythology. The song doesn't tell a story, though, as much as it fleshes out a portrait of a moment in time: Vikings on the sea, heading homeward after a five-year journey. The lyrics are unfortunately clunky at best, and the list of names of Norse warriors brings the Hammill oeuvre as close as it ever came to Spinal Tap territory. The music, though, is successful in portraying a sense of what the Vikings might have been feeling. It's worth noting that while Hammill's 'Refugees' are heading 'into the West', these Vikings are coming 'back from the West'.

Rod Clements, Martin Pottinger, and Ray Jackson, on bass, drums, and mandolin, respectively, have come over from side one to give the VdGG contingent (minus the other Jackson, who stays on) a well-deserved rest. Hammill and Fripp provide acoustic and electric guitars, respectively, and album cover artist Paul Whitehead joins in for the first of his two musical collaborations with Hammill (he would later play on the musique concrete extravaganza 'Magog (In Bromine Chambers)' on the 1974 *In Camera* album), playing the tam-tam, which is similar to a gong.

'The Birds' (Hammill)
Along with 'Vision', 'The Birds' enjoyed the most post- *Fool's Mate* longevity, remaining a staple of Hammill's live setlists to the present day. Evans, Potter, Banton, and Fripp provide the musical background to Hammill's excursion into extended metaphor (Banton is on piano; this is a rare instance of Hammill not playing an instrument on a solo album track). 'The Birds' is a simple song of profound ambivalence in a love affair. Like birds in early springtime who are surprised by a late frost, the narrator, brought up short by a sudden realisation that he is no longer in love with a partner for whom he had strong feelings only a few days prior, doesn't 'know which way to sing' – in sorrow for the loss or in celebration for newfound freedom?

'I Once Wrote Some Poems' (Hammill)
It's no accident that this song closes out the album. While of a piece with the rest of the material on *Fool's Mate*, 'I Once Wrote Some Poems' nevertheless is a quantum leap forward in terms of both Hammill's lyrical concerns and approach. It's a very stark musical landscape – only Hammill on acoustic

guitar – and Hammill's vocals are much more extreme on both ends, from the introductory whisper to the soul-baring climactic shout. This song would become a staple in Van der Graaf's live repertoire in 1971 and 1972; Hammill would play it alone to kick off the encore, and then fade into the wings as the rest of the band tore into the much more upbeat 'Theme One'. Signalling both the end of the song and the end of the album, Fripp reprises the sustained and feedback-laden three-note series that he played at the beginning of 'Imperial Zeppelin', but for a much longer duration. It lasts for 34 seconds, and the microtonal harmonics that fluctuate and waver are as hauntingly exquisite as the dissonance is jarring. It can be read any number of ways but was most likely intended as a bit of perverse humour and an acknowledgement and reminder that the previous 45 minutes were a deliberately artificial (in the best sense of the word) reconstruction of another time, and not the present state of play as far as Hammill was musically concerned.

2005 Reissue CD Bonus Tracks
'Re-Awakening' (Hammill)
'Summer Song (In the Autumn)' (Hammill)
'The Birds' (Hammill)
'Sunshine' (Hammill)
'Happy' (Hammill)

These five tracks are demo versions, recorded in January 1971 and only discovered during the research that was undertaken in service of the remastering of the album. As a group, they are of considerably less fidelity than the final versions, but are nonetheless essential, intriguing, and edifying performances. Evidently, the instrumentation is limited to what can be provided by Hugh Banton, Guy Evans, David Jackson, Nic Potter, and Peter Hammill. None of the songs that – in their completed versions – featured other musicians are included here and, furthermore, there is no Fripp. Aside from a slightly looser performance by all involved, the only real difference is the inclusion of Jackson's horn playing in 'The Birds', making the middle instrumental section quite a bit jazzier than the final version.

Pawn Hearts (1971)

Personnel:

Hugh Banton: Farfisa and Hammond organs, ARP synthesizer, Mellotron, bass guitar, vocals, bass pedals, electric razor

Guy Evans: drums, timpani, percussion, piano

Robert Fripp: electric guitar

Peter Hammill: lead vocals, acoustic and slide guitar, piano, electric piano

David Jackson: alto, tenor and soprano saxophones, flute, vocals, effects

Produced at Trident Studios, July – September 1971 by John Anthony.

UK release date and label: October 1971; Charisma. US release date and label: 1971, Charisma.

Highest chart places: Italy: 1.

Running time: 45:08

In October 1971, VdGG released what many believe to be their finest album, *Pawn Hearts*. In three sweeping pieces – one an epic study in the effects of isolation that stretches across an entire LP side – the band managed to forever confound facile definitions of what constitutes progressive rock. The original intent was for *Pawn Hearts* to be even more sprawling: a double album that would contain the three new songs on one disc, a third side comprising 'solo' efforts by each band member save Hammill, and a fourth side of live performances of earlier songs. This fourth side was to consist of fan-favourites from past tours: 'Darkness', 'Killer', and an extended suite that included 'Giant Squid' and 'Octopus'. Of these, only the latter survived in recorded format, and was added as a bonus track to the 2005 reissue of *H to He*. Charisma was not in a financial position to give their blessing to this idea, however, and so, perhaps for the better, what was pressed to vinyl and sent out into the world was the leaner and more focused set of three songs.

Van der Graaf Generator had been heading into more and more intricate and complex musical territory since the band's inception, but the jump from 1970's *H to He* to 1971's *Pawn Hearts* was nothing short of quantum. The band members all agree, in retrospect, that it was largely the intense amount of touring in the months leading up to the making of *Pawn Hearts* that pushed them to such extreme levels of creativity. Tony Stratton-Smith had encouraged them to tour Europe in the latter half of 1970 with other acts that were on the Charisma label, including Genesis and Lindisfarne. The tour was successful enough that Stratton-Smith urged them to tour again in early 1971 – this time in Germany.

Germany turned out to be not quite as hospitable or receptive to Van der Graaf's music as other parts of Europe had been, and the chaotic nature of life on the road without a stable cash flow – Charisma apparently had trouble wiring money to the band – drove the VdGG members to look for extraordinary ways to cope, and the angst and pressure were channelled (mainly for Hammill) into songwriting. It was during Hammill's downtime, hiding out on the bus, that he composed the album side-long epic suite 'A

Plague of Lighthouse-Keepers'.

Before 'Plague' came into being, however, the new album's other two lengthy cuts were written on the road – offered up in skeletal form by Hammill for the rest of the band to add to and arrange. First 'Lemmings', and then 'Man-Erg', were fleshed out and road-tested in concerts during the tour. 'Plague', by contrast, wasn't developed by the band until after the tour, and was the last thing VdGG worked on before going to record the album.

Just before the album was released, Stratton-Smith decided that *Pawn Hearts* needed a bit of a pop infusion, and – without informing the band – arranged to have 'Theme One' added to the disc – a decision the band was not happy with. Hammill, in particular, was enraged; he felt that an essential energy that had been built up by 'Lemmings' was prevented from flowing into 'Man-Erg' by the capricious insertion of the short, jaunty instrumental tune into the middle of the first side.

Fittingly for such a monumentally and ambitiously strange album, the cover artwork was eye-catching in its otherworldly splendour. Paul Whitehead took the cover art game for VdGG to the next level. He got the idea for the figures floating in the Earth's atmosphere inside a combination of a chess piece and a spacesuit from Hammill, who told him a bit about the concept behind the album, that underneath any exterior societal trappings of royalty or the elite, we're all pawns at heart. The scrim that is arcing and unfurling through the atmosphere, providing the illusion of a peaceful, cloud-festooned blue sky as a backdrop, and also apparently hiding the reality of cold and infinite space, came to Whitehead after listening to 'A Plague of Light-House Keepers'.

The remastered CD version of *Pawn Hearts* that was released in 2005 contained a number of 'extras' that will be discussed here following the essential three tracks that comprised the initial release. They include both sides of the single released some months after the album, as well as the three songs composed by the individual members of the band, minus Hammill, that was originally slated to be side four of the double album that the band had at first envisioned. As mentioned earlier, the 'live in studio' tracks that were slated for side three were lost to time, save for the 'Squid/Octopus' medley, which resurfaced on the 2005 reissue of *H to He Who Am the Only One*.

'Lemmings' (Hammill)

'Lemmings' opens the album, giving the uninitiated listener little warning or time to adjust before the reality-warping, lurching tune kicks in and accompanies Hammill's obliquely dystopian narrative. It starts with a sound of swirling wind similar to that which ushers in 'Darkness' on the album *The Least We Can Do*. Along with this sound effect, Hammill picks out a steady progression of notes on acoustic guitar, and Banton provides an insistent bass pulse on his organ; he and Jackson also provide short bursts and trills on their keyboards and sax and flute, respectively, as Hammill launches into the song's first few vocal lines. The lyrics' portent and gravitas increase as Banton's chords go up note by note and Evans brings the drums.

The band hits its stride at this point, homing in on the song's central riff, which they'll return to frequently throughout the duration, and it's here where the lyric shifts from the protagonist who opened the song to the voice that is presently described ('the voice, as one, as no-one, came to me'). This riff, which alternates with a marginally more sedate and reflective chord progression, goes on for a few minutes, reaching just past the end of the lyrical quote, and the subsequent repetition of and response to the question that the disembodied voice finishes with: 'What cause is there left but to die…?'

What follows is a series of departures, moving further out by degrees, from the comparative normality of the composition to this point, before finally returning to the now-familiar lurch. Here we hear faint but menacing animalistic bleats and moans courtesy of Jackson's devices, as well as more hints of that trademark wind, as Hammill's acoustic guitar carries the song into a brief lyrical riposte to The Voice, time enough for Hammill to embellish his bandmates' efforts with a few bloodcurdling shrieks. As with many musical asides on this album, it doesn't wear out its welcome and is replaced, at the 5-minute mark, by the sound of guitar strings being slowly mauled by a slide while time seems to freeze, ending in a flourish of multi-tracked noise resulting from the guitar neck and other assorted keyboard-related feedback. But the journey through the lemming-eye looking glass is just getting underway.

The middle section of 'Lemmings' – which earns its own title: 'Cog' – contains VdGG's freest playing and the most complete embrace of noise up to this point, and Robert Fripp is there to add his particular brand of unholy electric guitar chaos to the mix, playing very much in the style of his 'Sailor's Tale' guitar workout on King Crimson's 1971 *Islands* album.

Not before time, the song abruptly halts its relentless forward charge, as though it were a horde of lemmings reaching the cliff edge, and Evans and Banton take the tune into a beautiful, twinkling free fall, peppering the darkness with gentle cymbal sweeps and keyboard flourishes before Jackson joins in on flute, and Evans closes the track out with a percussive 'thunk'. Banton confirms that not only did Fripp play in the 'Cog' section of the song, he also provided some guitar work to be overdubbed at the conclusion of 'Lemmings', but a decision was made to leave it in the studio.

'Man-Erg' (Hammill)

In contrast to 'Lemmings', 'Man-Erg' is a very orderly piece of music, with clearly defined sections. Where 'Lemmings' seemed to skitter and scramble, 'Man-Erg' strides with purpose. Which just makes the inevitable lunatic interlude (this IS VdGG after all) more effective. On piano instead of guitar, Hammill leads the band through the opening part of the song, singing of killers and angels that 'live inside' him, until about the three-minute mark, at which point the floor gives way and the band maniacally pound out a frenetic riff that finds Jackson and Banton furiously honking and pounding away, with Evans steering and Hammill reporting from the front lines of a cataclysmic existential crisis. Spent, finally (the audience and the musicians, likely), the band wheels around and carries the song into a calmer, jazzier area – post-nervous breakdown with a lilt! More swinging and jazz-tinged playing follows, with some lovely horn work from Jackson and soloing from Fripp, again, before the song's opening theme is revisited, with a good deal more gravitas, after which the band launch into a heavy and extremely satisfying conclusion, ending the first side of this legendary album. 'Man-Erg' survived beyond the VdGG split in 1978 and appeared in Hammill setlists until the early 1980s. The main theme that runs through the lyrics to the song eventually came to inspire the title of the first collected volume of Hammill's writings, *Killers, Angels, Refugees*.

'A Plague of Lighthouse-Keepers' (Banton, Evans, Hammill, Jackson)

Although 'Lemmings' and 'Man-Erg' both became VdGG classics, they were overshadowed by their grander sibling, the immense and imposing ten-part 'A Plague of Lighthouse-Keepers'. When 'Plague' was complete and safely on tape, Hammill reportedly felt as if everything he and the band had been working towards, in terms of expression, had been fulfilled. The rest of the band knew that they had created something incredible, but weren't sure how it was going to go over. The fact of the matter was that critics, and many of their fans, didn't know quite what to do with *Pawn Hearts*, and that was largely down to the relative inaccessibility of 'Plague'.

The lyrical theme, on the surface, is about a lighthouse keeper who has entered into an existential crisis – haunted by the souls of the seafarers that he has been unable to save, and by his own perpetual loneliness. In an interview with *Sounds* at the time of the album's release, and referenced in Christopulos and Smart's book, Hammill explained that it went deeper: on another level, the narrator was facing and dealing with his own psyche, and there were also elements of a coming-to-terms with society. The ten parts of 'Plague' are subtitled as follows:

'Eyewitness' (Hammill)
'Pictures / Lighthouse' (Banton, Hammill)
'Eyewitness' (Hammill)
'S. H. M'. (Hammill)
'Presence of the Night' (Hammill)
'Kosmos Tours' (Evans)
'(Custard's) Last Stand' (Hammill)
'The Clot Thickens' (Hammill, Banton, Evans, Jackson)
'Land's End (Sineline)' (Jackson)
'We Go Now' (Banton, Jackson)

While Hammill provided the basic structure underlying the work, other band members came up with various sections: Banton wrote some of the music for 'Pictures / Lighthouse,' Evans came up with the keyboard part that underpinned 'Kosmos Tours', and Jackson wrote the closing section, 'We Go Now'. None of these sections have ever appeared as standalones on record, although a medley consisting of 'Eyewitness' and 'The Clot Thickens' was regularly performed in concert by the final iteration of Van der Graaf, and subsequently for a number of years by Hammill in a solo context, until it dropped off the setlist in the early 1980s.

'Eyewitness' starts the proceedings off in a mellow and introspective mood, with electric piano chord stabs courtesy of Hammill, organ bass pedals, and Hammill's foreboding croon accompanied by gentle sax tones from Jackson. The first quatrain is sung in a hesitant, cautious-sounding voice, followed by two more in a decidedly different voicing bordering on falsetto, that subtly carries the song into a more dynamic and turbulent field of sound. At this point, Evans joins in on drums, and an insistent riff emerges from Banton's keyboard. Hammill's narration continues with a fourth quatrain delivered in a much more ominous voice that sounds like it may be coming through a bullhorn or some other form of amplification that wouldn't be out of place in a lighthouse keeper's arsenal. It's the fourth voicing, though, in these series of characterisations that serve to portray the narrator as psychically fragmented, that truly gives an indication of there being something 'off'. Not only does this voice sound manically unhinged with its odd syllabic emphases and departures from the notes that have been established as the vocal melody, but there is an unholy chorus of background vocals (Hammill, of course) echoing the narrator's words in a deranged falsetto. Here, Banton overlays an additional discordant organ flourish to accentuate the transgressive intrusion.

Following this hair-raising bit, the band bears down in a more familiar VdGG vibe, with Hammill sounding more in control, but more menacing, as the narrator directly addresses the listener: 'When you see the skeletons of sailing-ship spars sinking low / You'll begin to wonder if the points of all the ancient myths are solemnly directed straight at you.' All of this so far in under two and a half minutes!

As Hammill's last held note and Banton's organ riff fade into the distance, the second section of 'Plague', 'Pictures / Lighthouse' kicks in. It's an atmospheric and proto-ambient interlude that attempts to sonically represent a lighthouse keeper's (and ship captain's) worst fear: an imminent collision. We hear a flurry of notes, far off in the sonic field from Jackson on flute and sax, likely representing gulls' cries, over a subtly unassuming but persistent electronic tone from Banton, generating an unease that plays at odds with the birdcalls. As the latter fades and the former rises in volume, Jackson comes back with a series of powerful amplified sax blasts that sound like a maritime warning siren, growing in volume and intensity until at last, they're at ground zero in the sonic field, and Jackson actually uses two saxophones simultaneously, in different octaves, to increase the urgency and fearsomeness of the warning to a degree that's almost disorienting. This onslaught is followed by an equally catastrophic-sounding drum rampage from Evans that pans across the stereo landscape (or seascape/shoreline) mimicking the sound of collision as well as perhaps the wrath of a vengeful deity overseeing a storm-tossed stretch of sea.

This is only the first of two parts of the instrumental interlude (likely corresponding to the split title). As the sonic field slowly shifts away from the apparent carnage, Banton engages in a meditative and calming organ solo that very gradually rises in volume and (musical) scale until it achieves a euphoric peak. The interlude closes out with a return to the now-established organ riff of 'Eyewitness' as we enter a reprise of the first part of 'Plague'.

In the return to the opening theme, the riff and vocal melody are briefly repeated – another quatrain – before the tempo increases and the music becomes frenetic. The narrator signals a descent into madness, apparently brought on by a combination of solitude and monotony. Banton briefly introduces another organ riff which Jackson complements, and the two musicians bring us into the fourth section of 'Plague', 'S. H. M'.

The acronym that serves as this section's title refers, according to Banton, to 'simple harmonic motion', the model used in physics to describe the effect that a 'restoring force' has on a moving object, like a pendulum, or a plucked guitar string, moving the object back towards its starting point with a force equal to that which propels it. One can only guess why this was chosen as the title for this section, but it seems to echo the sense of to and fro typified by waves breaking on a shore, and more specifically, the push and pull of the fractured portions of the narrator's psyche that encounter the phantasms described in the lyrics: 'The spectres scratch on window-slits / the hollowed faces and mindless grins / are only intent on destroying what they've lost'.

'S. H. M.' is a rollicking piece of music; for the first six and a half minutes of 'Plague', the band has been somewhat restrained, and now, with Hammill's shouts of 'Unreal! Unreal!' caution is thrown to the salty sea-spray that flies about Jackson's ebullient parping and Banton's ringing organ tones. In a sharp contrast to the apocalyptic vibe of the lyrics, the music at this point positively swings – but it's not entirely without menace, especially as the section winds down.

The next section, 'Presence of the Night', has in itself two parts. The first is comparatively minimalist and achingly gorgeous. It begins with dual keyboards from Hammill (electric piano) and Banton (organ), and gentle sax and vocals. Hammill's vocal contribution is a brief four lines, but it's perhaps the torchiest singing he'd done to date. He's replaced in the piece by the band's secret weapon of a guest musician, Robert Fripp, who once again provides some tasteful electric guitar embellishments. It's Banton's organ melody, though – simultaneously languorous and insistent – that makes this a hidden VdGG gem.

The band wouldn't produce anything nearly this tender or fragile again until 1976's 'My Room' on the *Still Life* album. Van der Graaf Generator, with Fripp, improvise over Banton's melodic riff, growing fainter until finally fading out completely, as Hammill re-enters with vocals recorded to give the impression of being deeply submerged. While the first part of 'Presence' has the narrator quoting the 'ghosts' that torment him, the second sees him again addressing the listener: 'Would you catch my words?' The band quickly regains steam with a dynamic approach that is alternately forceful and lilting, like a boxer's attack and retreat, backing the narrator's rhetorical thrusts and parrying when he falls silent before the next salvo. 'Presence' climaxes with the band going all out with a restatement of the theme of the second part that develops into a crescendo before segueing into the next section.

'Kosmos Tours' emerges from the end of 'Presence of the Night' as a wildly chaotic storm of keyboard riffs, recorded individually and layered one after another, to create a profoundly unsettling but thrilling minute-long piece of music. Evans, in Christopulos and Smart's book, states that he came up with the keyboard part and taught it to Banton, who played variations of it on the organ, with all manner of different settings, while Evans himself contributed the portion played on piano. Evans's drums can also be heard over the top of the wall of sound, along with Jackson's saxophone, and eventually, Hammill intones another short burst of vocals, appropriately referring to the inner turmoil that the narrator is experiencing as a 'maelstrom'. 'Kosmos' finishes with an abrupt crash of a piano chord.

After a few seconds of silence, 'Plague' picks up again with the next section, the groan-inducingly titled '(Custard's) Last Stand'. This section is the most conventionally pop song-like part of the suite, with parts that behave somewhat like verses and choruses butting up against each other. In each case, however (three quasi-verse structures to two quasi-choruses), it's more of a thought reaching an emphatic conclusion.

Just as the end of 'Eyewitness' signals the imminent madness depicted in 'S.H.M', the climax of '(Custard's) Last Stand' prefigures the profound existential crisis in the next section, 'The Clot Thickens' (extending the titular pun). Without warning, the band explode into a furiously paced gallop through an equally unexpected vocal minefield. Hammill's narrator barks out frantic questions which indicate his perilous position in a psychic whirlpool: 'Where is the God that guides my hand? How can the hands of others reach me? When will I find what I grope for? Who is going to teach me?' The words 'where', 'God', 'how', when' and 'grope' from these lyrics are superimposed over the main vocal, in a terrifyingly distorted and machine-like perversion of the original, giving the disorienting sense of another consciousness looking down on the scene in which the narrator has centre stage. And that gets at the heart of the whole suite: the narrator has been experiencing himself – the 'I' and 'me' – as two (or more) discrete entities, and also sees his singular self as a plural 'we' comprised of parts that are at odds with one another.

'Clot' continues on with increasing musical chaos as Banton introduces a mellotron to the sonic canvas. In sharp contrast to the mellotron's usual role as a sombre becalming agent in the realm of late 1960s/early 1970s progressive-leaning rock, Banton uses the instrument to project a sense of disorientation and unease, as though the chords were waves tossing the listener around on the sea. It's worth noting that VdGG compatriot Robert Fripp's band, King Crimson, used the mellotron to similar effect in the similarly nautical-themed instrumental piece 'The Devil's Triangle', found on their 1970 album *In the Wake of Poseidon*, as well as that record's title track. Also, interestingly, as Hammill's narrator approaches the limits of what he seems to be able to endure, he references the first two songs on the album – 'I can see the lemmings coming, but I know I'm just a man' – thus bringing the whole of 'Pawn Hearts' together as a unified statement.

The storm that VdGG has been brewing abruptly ceases along with 'The Clot Thickens', replaced by the calm and evenly paced penultimate section of 'Plague', 'Land's End (Sineline)'. The sine wave reference brings us back to the scientific principle of 'simple harmonic motion' that was alluded to in the second part of the suite; the meaning here is as elusive and elliptical as it was earlier, but seems to indicate the presence of an equilibrium that was previously lacking. The first half of this tune features Hammill almost completely by himself on piano and near-falsetto vocals, accompanied only by Banton's faint splashes of colour and Evans's quietly restrained drum taps in the background. As the third verse begins, Banton and Evans join in on the foreground, accompanying Hammill on a final push, partly celebratory and partly yearning, towards the horizon. The presence of several distinct voices that marked the earlier 'Eyewitness' section resurfaces here – although the voices don't sound that dissimilar, the verses overlap with the next starting before the previous one is finished, giving the impression of a series of speakers taking their turn in the spotlight. We're left with a sense that the narrator has found peace, though it's unclear whether his disparate selves have been reunified or are existing separately in harmony, as Hammill closes with the Zen koan-like final tercet: 'All things are a part / All things are apart / All things are a part'.

'Plague' closes with a triumphant instrumental piece titled 'We Go Now', that, like the previous section, doesn't include any contributions from Jackson. This is especially odd given that he's credited as having come up with this tune, which was the seed that eventually grew into 'A Plague of Lighthouse-Keepers'. The rest of the band shine, however, as piano merges with multiple organ parts and a choir of overdubbed wordless vocals from Hammill. Evans's cymbals, sounding like static interference, soar over the top as the epic suite slowly fades out.

'Theme One' (George Martin)

Some early pressings of the album contained a fourth track that was intended to be released as a single; the band's rendition of the then-ubiquitous BBC broadcast closer, composed by Sir George Martin and not-so-imaginatively titled 'Theme One'. In contrast to the portentous atmosphere created by much of the three main album tracks, this instrumental is infectiously catchy and full of a different kind of intensity. It manages to aim for the usual VdGG targets that sit beyond the barriers separating the everyday world from the zone of inspired lunacy, while trading seriousness for unadulterated fun.

During the shows VdGG played prior to the release of *Pawn Hearts*, they began to encore with oddball selections from outside their catalogue, with the intent of diffusing some of the dark and intense energy that their main set had built up. The band often heard the official version of 'Theme One' on the car radio while driving in the very early morning, and it worked its way into their hearts – before long, it became their signature closing song. Hammill would appear on stage first for the encore, perform his song, 'I Once Wrote Some Poems', and then fade into the wings as the other three members took the spotlight and tore into the 'Theme'.

'w' (Hammill)

'w' was released as the B-side to the 'Theme One' single in February, 1972. The lyrics were written by Hammill and date back to his university days, and share a kinship with previous VdGG songs like 'House with No Door' and 'Out of My Book', but with a healthy dollop of morbid humour and surrealism thrown in. 'w' is a strange tune, even by VdGG standards, and at only a little over four minutes, which in itself is strange for Van der Graaf, the oddness seems magnified.

The song begins with a drone-like instrumental passage played by Jackson and Banton. When the playing coalesces into song-form, Hammill begins to intone the lyrics in a slow and dreamy fashion befitting the song's exploration of liminal states of consciousness. The middle of the song contains a passage of entirely free, improvised playing, which was new to VdGG, at least in the area of recorded output.

'Angle of Incidents' (Evans)

The first of the three 'solo' tracks appended to the 2005 reissue, 'Angle of Incidents' displays Guy Evans's interest in contemporary avant-garde music. The track features a wildly experimental approach to percussion, including a backwards recording of Evans's drumming as well as the sound of fluorescent bulbs being thrown down a stairwell in Trident Studios, according to Mark Powell in the liner notes to the 2005 *Pawn Hearts* reissue.

'Angle of Incidents' also features some wild saxophone from David Jackson and a bit of understated keyboard accompaniment from Hugh Banton. Much of what transpires here sounds like an antecedent to the musique concrete found in 'Magog (In Bromine Chambers)' on Peter Hammill's 1974 album *In Camera*, including the whistling sound of objects being swung about, and spoken vocals (origin unknown) that are played back at a vastly reduced speed.

'Ponker's Theme' (Jackson)

Since 'Archimedes Agnostic', the longer composition that David Jackson intended to use for side four of 'Pawn Hearts', has been lost to time, Jackson's only solo representation here is the brief and slight jazz tune 'Ponker's Theme', clocking in at one and a half minutes. Jackson, Banton and Evans deliver an innocuous compliment to 'Theme One', with the drums skittering all over and playing havoc with the tempo, while the bass (Banton on pedals) chugs along and the piano rounds out the jazz combo vibe. Parallels become more obvious towards the song's end, as the trio engage in a rave-up that is very similar to the one at the climax of 'Theme One'.

'Diminutions' (Banton)

Hugh Banton's contribution to the aborted solo section of *Pawn Hearts* is really just him alone, with multi-layered organ parts, unlike Evans's and Jackson's tracks, which were performed by the Hammill-less trio. 'Diminutions', like its counterparts, is tied to other extant pieces of VdGG-related music. In this case, it's the 'Pictures / Lighthouse' section of 'A Plague of Lighthouse Keepers'. Both pieces use the layering approach to build on what's been played, but while the 'Plague' section does so in ever-increasing intensity, leading to a euphoric climax, 'Diminutions' remains coolly placid and remote – it's lovely but not exactly rousing.

Chameleon in the Shadow of the Night (1973)

Personnel:
Hugh Banton: Hammond organ, piano, bass
Guy Evans: drums
Peter Hammill: vocals, acoustic and electric guitars, Mellotron, piano, harmonium
David Jackson: alto and tenor saxophone, flute
Nic Potter: bass
Produced at Rockfield Studios, March 1973, by John Anthony and Peter Hammill
UK release date and label: May 1973; Charisma. US release date and label: 1989, Caroline.

In May 1973, Peter Hammill released what many consider to be his first 'proper' solo album, as the earlier *Fool's Mate* was essentially a collection of older songs that deserved to be heard but wasn't really indicative of Hammill's artistic stance at the time it was released. By contrast, *Chameleon in the Shadow of the Night* is a work very much of its time, showcasing not only Hammill's growing musical prowess and technical savvy in the studio, but also painting a vibrant, if melancholy, picture of the time and situation he (and other members of VdGG) found themselves in.

As dismal as band-life had become, dealing with its dissolution was, in some ways, harder, at least for Hammill. That sort of post-partum sadness permeates the songs on the album, along with a recurring sense of indecision and self-recrimination. The album's title sums up quite well – the overall feeling that the album generates – a disappearing into one's surroundings, as a chameleon does, but in this case, it's more than outward camouflage; the night provides a cover that ensures, even allows, the figure in question to disappear from their own view, into nothingness.

It's not easy at first to tell the difference between solo Hammill work from the early 1970s and Van der Graaf Generator. The VdGG musicians are present, and the style of music is somewhat similar. The difference is – aside from the fact that there are quite a few songs on the solo albums in question where the only player is Hammill – that Peter is the ultimate decision-maker. These are his songs, on his albums. Where he would usually bring songs in some stage of completion to fellow band members to work out and fine-tune for a VdGG album, on the solo albums, there was little input. The other former band members were there as supporting musicians, to play the material, rather than as co-creators. Hammill has said often in interviews in more recent decades that he thoroughly appreciates the opportunity to record as guest guitarist or vocalist on someone else's album because he is then freed from responsibility for the final outcome and can simply enjoy playing or singing without fretting about the final result. It's likely that the reverse is true, and that when you hear Evans, Banton, Jackson, and even Potter, playing alongside Hammill in the studio on *Chameleon*, you can safely assume they're having fun.

'German Overalls' (Hammill)

The opening track on *Chameleon* is just Hammill, but the sonics are quite wide-ranging. While the song mostly hinges on his acoustic guitar playing, the use of organ and manipulation of both feedback and vocals makes for a deliciously trippy listening experience, as far out as the strangest VdGG forays, if much starker. The subject matter, though, is bleak: decidedly autobiographical, it documents VdGG's last touring days in Germany, even referring to Banton and Jackson by name. Throughout the song, Hammill attempts to process the confusion and alienation that were by-products of life in a band constantly on tour, and the climax is just a heightened and paradoxically clear sense of the confusion he's experiencing.

'Slender Threads' (Hammill)

Peter and his guitar, and an avalanche-worth of guilt and despair. This lovely and understated tune is an interpersonal song, one of many to come that would examine the state of a romantic relationship – where it stands, and more interestingly, where and how it may have stopped working. Some soliloquising and ruminating ensues, leading to a panicked and early climax in the song: 'Yes, and I wonder if I'm gonna make it through the night!' A rhetorical concern, of course. The song ends with a morbid curiosity regarding whether a hand offered to help 'save' the person in question might unwittingly prove to be the agent of her demise.

'Rock and Role' (Hammill)

After an increasingly narrow sonic field, the third track opens up to surprise first-time listeners with an abundance of noise from Hammill's electric guitar shenanigans, Nic Potter's bass, Guy Evans's drums (both rumbling tremendously), and David Jackson's saxophone – the four old bandmates punch their vehicle into overdrive. Hammill's vocals soar over everything, up to an early middle section, where things slow down, and piano (Hammill, again) is introduced to the mix. Here, the vocals adopt a treated, loudspeaker-like quality – the whooping war cry becomes omniscient, though not for long – the ex-VdGG contingent can't be kept down, and they buck their way into a slightly accelerated version of the first go-round, for another onslaught, before finally settling into an edgy groove, improvising against the melody as the song slowly fades. 'Rock and Role' is significant as it gives a preview of the trio dynamic (Hammill, Evans, and Potter) that would provide the base for a portion of the 1977 solo album, *Over*, and in fact, in touring behind that album, these three, along with Graham Smith on violin, would make this song a centrepiece of their concerts.

'In the End' (Hammill)

Stripping things back down to one person, but with piano replacing guitar, Hammill gives us his marathonic throwing down of the gauntlet. With different words and approaches, many of the same questions that were posited in 'German Overalls' are being repeated, but in a much less passive way. Hammill was content to drift and comment with some remove on his situation; by contrast, this seems like a do-or-die crossroads. The song's title seems to focus on a distant future, but the lyrics are very much about situations in the present and the immediate future. The singer is about to act, and the stakes are high, and he knows that the analysis is as necessary as breathing, but also as unlikely to change whatever course is set. Seven minutes of piano keyboard abuse and a sustained, coruscating delivery, the fury and intensity of which we've not yet heard from Hammill, makes for an intense listening experience that is as discomfiting as it is satisfying.

'What's It Worth' (Hammill)

A simpler tune opens side B of *Chameleon*. 'What's It Worth' is lighter in intensity and mood and it is yet another kick at the dust that's settled around Hammill post-VdGG and threatens to accrue further, perhaps obscuring the qualities that make life special and engaging. Puns and wordplay abound in the lyrics, and while it's clear that this song is yet another in this album's collection of examinations of the present state of things, musically it feels like a close cousin to the much of the material on the previous solo album, *Fool's Mate* in its easy, pastoral flow. 'What's It Worth' entered the realm of live performance by Hammill in the late 'noughts', and has been a reliably constant component of his concerts in the last decade.

'Easy to Slip Away' (Hammill)

As Hammill picks out the opening notes to this song on the piano, the listener might be wondering if they're back in 'Refugees' or 'House with No Door' territory. Jackson's sax playing might further complicate perceptions, but the listener will soon realise that this primarily piano-based song has sax, bass, and even Mellotron accompaniment, but is emphatically not a band song. That said, there are some very intricate parts near the middle of the piece. Here, Hammill's voice is incredibly emotive without needing to go full-throttle; there is just enough depth to infuse its emotionality with a dreary beauty that powerfully evokes the feeling of youthful loss that occurs when one leaves the closest of friends behind.

Complicating this song's relation to the past VdGG canon is the fact that this is the second song, after 'Refugees', to namecheck 'Mike' and 'Susie' (along with the lyric, 'The refugees are gone'.) Where they existed in the lyrics of the earlier song as a pair, here they are treated individually – first Susie, then Mike – each addressed by the singer in an imaginary apology for disappearing from their lives. We know, now, who these characters are, and to drive the point home, clues to Susie's identity, at least, are dropped by way of bits of information about her vocation.

Despite the complex instrumentation, this song works quite well arranged for solo piano, and of all the songs on *Chameleon*, it's the one that's been played live the most in a solo context. The 2006 reissue of this album includes a bonus live recording of 'Easy to Slip Away' from the same performance where the bonus live recording of 'In the End' is sourced.

'Dropping the Torch' (Hammill)

Another solo acoustic guitar number, 'Dropping the Torch' stands in stark contrast to its Side B companion piece, 'What's It Worth'. While the latter is a light, gentle poke at the singer's existential predicament, the former is existentialist with a capital E. Prescriptive, and with no small amount of archness, 'Dropping the Torch' laments what is described as an inevitable occurrence: the loss of free will to the outcome of ever more dicey cause and effect pairings; it's a seemingly insurmountable dilemma that we're faced with: in trying to protect the spark that represents our existence, we become overly cautious and, in a gamble for security, end up extinguishing that very spark, finding that our safety zone, is, in fact, an airless room.

'(In the) Black Room' (Hammill)

Written for VdGG and rehearsed and performed with the band during the last days of touring before the split, this sprawling, and brawling, prog suite was already pretty much fully formed at the time of the *Chameleon* recording sessions. Although it was augmented slightly for use on a solo, as opposed to a band, album, Hammill claims that 'the arrangement here is very close to the VdGG one'. As VdGG would again make 'Black Room' a staple of their live shows upon their reformation in 1975, distinguishing the piece as a solo song or a band song is almost academic. In discussing its provenance, in the 2006 liner notes, Hammill makes the distinction clear, both for this instance and in the case of any questions of solo/band provenance: 'though personnel are identical, he whose project it is gets both the responsibility and the choice when it comes to decisions'.

With a noise guaranteed to make first-time listeners jump, the entire classic VdGG line-up, plus Nic Potter, jumpstart the proceedings, following the tiny, plaintive vocal that closes the previous track. After the 'Umbraceous Ensemble' (as they are classified in the liner notes on the original gatefold LP) re-introduce themselves, things get going in spectacular VdGG fashion: the stops and starts, sudden 90-degree turns, and tightly, if strangely, interlocking riffs. Perhaps because it is, finally, a Hammill song, it is constantly countering the flights and meanderings into bizarre territory with reins that pull the beast back into the world of rock and roll. And through all of Jackson's squealing and honking and Banton's organ wizardry (but also doubling on bass guitar, rather than the usual bass pedals, something he was doing more and more), Hammill revisits some of the themes of the album's opener, 'German Overalls'. But where that track was lyrically concerned with the exterior life, 'Black Room' investigates the interior.

Rejecting the easy promise of LSD, Hammill decided to undergo an attempt at something like brain-change, but focuses lyrically on mysticism rather than psychology. The situating of the conscious mind in the 'black room' of the egoless self is meant to allow the experimenter to see reality unfettered by preconceptions – and this is what the listener is presented with in 'The Tower' – cosmic but primal images, with a horrific hue, that terrify the experimenter and lead to the epiphanic key that returns us to (the second part of) 'Black Room' for a brief but glorious fist-pumping anthem if there ever was one. Compare this victory whoop to the relatively calm sense of conclusion at the end of 'A Plague of Lighthouse-Keepers', and you'll see that this is ultimately the work of one man and not, for better or worse, music that was completed by consensus.

2006 Remastered CD Bonus Tracks
'Rain 3AM' (Hammill)

A song lost to time, and first released on a Virgin/Charisma label Hammill compilation, *The Calm (Before the Storm)*. Banton recorded the session, which features Hammill on piano and guitar, with David Jackson on flute, during the time of the *Silent Corner and the Empty Stage* sessions in 1973. It sounds like it would have fit as easily on *Fool's Mate* as *Chameleon*, likely because it was written in the same period as most of the other *Fool's Mate* songs, in 1967. Oddly, though, it wasn't originally intended for either.

'Easy to Slip Away (live)' (Hammill)
'In the End (live)' (Hammill)

These two bonus tracks were recorded during a legendary solo Hammill performance from 16 February, 1978 at the All Souls Unitarian Church in Kansas City. This concert was available first on vinyl and then CD as a bootleg titled *Skeletons of Songs*. With the re-release campaign of the Virgin/Charisma Hammill solo albums, some of the songs from this performance have been included where contextually appropriate.

The Silent Corner and the Empty Stage (1974)

Personnel:
Hugh Banton: organ, bass, vocals
Randy California: lead guitar
Guy Evans: drums
Peter Hammill: vocals, acoustic and electric guitars, bass, piano, harmonium,
Mellotron, oscillator
David Jackson: alto, soprano and tenor saxophones, flute
Produced at Trident Studios, October 1973, by John Anthony and Peter Hammill.
UK release date and label: February 1974; Charisma. US release date and label:
1990, Caroline
Running time: 49:50

The year 1974 is held in especially high esteem for many Hammill fans, and for good reason: it saw the release of not one, but two spectacularly impressive albums that, though released very early in an incredibly prolific career, remain high-water marks by which, rightly or wrongly, future albums would always be judged.

The first of the two, *The Silent Corner and the Empty Stage*, has, like its predecessor, a fair amount of completely solo performances but, here, Hammill can be seen extending his range of instrumentation and making more use of multi-track recording. Some of the album was recorded by Hammill in his home studio, in September and October of 1973. 'The Lie', 'Forsaken Gardens', and 'A Louse Is Not a Home' were recorded with Hammill's former bandmates at Rockfield Studios.

Bettina Hohls, the German artist responsible for the photographs that graced the cover and inner gatefold of *Chameleon in the Shadow of the Night*, did the artwork for *Silent Corner*, capturing, with hallucinogenic incisiveness, thematic elements common to all the songs.

'Modern' (Hammill)

The opening track, 'Modern', is, above all, angry. Acoustic guitar chords cut swathes through the overgrowth of urban spaces, both real and metaphorical. Backed by eventual bass (here, Hammill's performance is particularly savage), electric guitar and Mellotron, but no drums, the song's blueprint leaves sufficient space for it to be successfully reinterpreted, as it has been over the years, by many different band line-ups post VdGG and solo re-imaginations. The lion's share of the song was recorded in Hammill's home studio; Mellotron and vocals were added at Rockfield Studios.

After two quick verses, and a sort of middle-eight, 'Modern' veers off into deliciously sinister territory, with the already-established acoustic guitar attack butting up against washes of Mellotron and precisely timed pulses of electric guitar feedback. Cutting back, we find ourselves in a third verse, enhanced by the Mellotron and electric guitar that had been introduced in the interim, and a slow fade-out that stands in stark contrast to the song's sudden beginning. According to Hammill, this was his first complex solo composition that didn't lend itself to the Van der Graaf Generator musical realm.

'Wilhelmina' (Hammill)

Narrowing the social critique to an interpersonal rather than municipal level, Hammill presents us with a song of advice directed at a young girl. 'Wilhelmina' was written for Guy Evans's daughter – Evans was the first of any of the VdGG members to start a family. Although her given name is not Wilhelmina, Evans states, they hadn't decided on a name right away when she was born, and for a short time she was known as 'Willie'. Despite not yet being a parent, Hammill writes from the perspective of one, adopting a 'we' persona that contrasts with the 'you' in the lyrics. Piano and Mellotron comprise the instrumentation, and 'Wilhelmina' ends up being a solid effort in the early days of Hammill's ballad-ish explorations of human nature. It's also a fine study of his early use of backing vocals as an instrument in itself. Legendary crooner Shirley Bassey came close to recording a cover version of the song shortly after the release of *Silent Corner*, but in the end it didn't happen, for reasons unknown.

'The Lie (Bernini's Saint Theresa)' (Hammill)

Another song built on piano and organ, with Banton on bass, here Hammill reclaims the fury that drove 'Modern', and pits it against religious hypocrisy, using the famous statue of Saint Teresa in ecstasy that was crafted by Gian Lorenzo Bernini in the mid-17th century as a metaphor. Piano reverb and organ tones really help to achieve the sound of being in a large cathedral. At times, as in the middle of the song, the chords are tremendously uplifting, but the slow creep of the song's finale, and the finale itself, are utterly terrifying – Hammill's vocals sound as if they're coming from some place other than his body, and there is a range of backing vocals that dip down into very low octaves. Mixed with the lingering tones of the keyboard, this makes for one of the most memorably hair-raising moments in Hammill's recorded oeuvre. Along with 'Modern', it's the other song from 'Silent Corner' that Hammill regularly revisits in live performances.

'Forsaken Gardens' (Hammill)

After the extreme interiority of the previous song, we're treated to a much more pastoral piece. 'Forsaken Gardens' is the closest we see and hear of what VdGG might have sounded like during the 1972-75 hiatus period. It opens with gentle vocals and piano chords that are reminiscent of 'Refugees' and 'House with No Door'. Jackson's arsenal of saxes and flute sounds considerably more advanced and refined, however – no lullabies, here, but not an electro-horn sonic attack either. Evans's drumming prefigures the crisp beat he would whip up from time to time on future VdGG albums like *Still Life*, and Banton, here, does triple-duty: organ, bass, and what's mysteriously referred to in the original album credits as 'part-choir', singing along with Hammill, as near as this author can tell, in the few vocal lines just before the extended instrumental break, which features an understated electric guitar presence – a la 'Rock and Role' – as well as all the other suspects. VdGG fans would hear this song in concert when the band reformed and toured in 1975.

'Red Shift' (Hammill)

This is a strange song, no matter how one looks at it. An anomaly among the songs recorded for 'Silent Corner', it was the only one recorded at Island Studios, rather than Hammill's home studio or the Charisma-friendly Rockfield Studios. Oddity #2: singer, guitarist, and principal songwriter for the US band Spirit, Randy California, played lead electric guitar, including solos, alongside Hammill's own idiosyncratic guitar work. Oh, and it's a song about 'scientific alienation', using the phenomenon of the redshift and its attendant ties to Einsteinian relativity as an analogy for the poetic conceit of falling uselessly to the outer edges of the universe that is comprised, paradoxically, of you.

The song is filled out with bass and drums from Banton and Evans, respectively, and sax from Jackson that fit the song precisely and still sounded like a transmission from another planet. In the liner notes to the remastered CD edition of *Silent Corner* re-released in 2006, Hammill states that 'Red Shift' is one of the earlier Hammill/Chris Judge Smith co-compositions, written in 1967.

'Rubicon' (Hammill)

Hammill's acoustic guitar, buttressed by some truly beautiful bass-playing by Banton, makes up the song here, save for some additional mellotron colouring from the former during the brief solo passage. Lyrically, it's a heartfelt, cajoling, but ultimately ambiguous plea to a lover to make the right choice, whether it's to go or stay, invoking the myth of the Rubicon, and noting that 'if you cross the stream, you never can return / if you stay, you'll surely burn'.

'A Louse Is Not a Home' (Hammill)

'Black Room' might have been a one-off, but here we have the beginning of a pattern, and perhaps even a trend towards closing solo albums with monstrously epic, senses-assaulting prog rock leviathans. 'Louse' is another song originally written for the VdGG album that would have followed *Pawn Hearts*. It would be incorporated into the band's live repertoire upon its reformation the following year. The song comprises twelve and a half minutes of Gothic horror tropes, and philosophical 'I'-hunting. Using a 'house' (in whatever shifting shape it may take during any point of the lyric) as an analogy for the superstructure that is one's overarching, highest self, while also the structure in which the part of the self that consciously processes its world resides, the song explores the inevitable cognitive dissonance that erupts when the 'I' that is the furtive and fearful house-dweller runs into the 'I' that is, in effect, the house.

All this is channelled through a simultaneously joyous and harrowing performance from the erstwhile members of VdGG. Jackson creates a particularly forbidding and memorable wall of sound with his flute and electrified three-horned 'altotenorandsoprano' (as the liner notes have it) sax attack, and Evans's masterful drumming brings a touch of the supernatural with artificially sped-up drum tracks. Banton, once again, does double duty on organ and bass, and Hammill gives an over-the-top vocal delivery that is often rapid-fire and linguistically astounding. And it comes down to Hammill, and the chilling electronic post-production of his own voice, making the word 'I', repeatedly intoned, become fractured and eventually dematerialised, in what has to be the most potent example of the dispersion of one's psyche.

Bonus tracks from the 2006 CD remastered version
'The Lie' (Hammill)
Another track recorded live in Kansas City in 1978, this version doesn't have all the creepy iciness afforded the studio version by the echo and reverb, but Hammill's utterly over-the-top performance here supplies the creep factor in spades. Breathtaking.

'Rubicon'
'Red Shift' (Hammill)
These two tracks were from a John Peel Session 'live in studio' BBC transmission that first aired 5 March 1974. They both featured Peter Hammill on vocals and acoustic guitar and David Jackson on flute ('Rubicon'), and saxophone ('Red Shift'). Hammill claims that this performance of 'Red Shift' hews much closer to the spirit of the original version (which was discussed above) than the more modern, California-enhanced take.

In Camera (1974)

Personnel:
Guy Evans: drums
Peter Hammill: vocals, acoustic and electric guitars, bass guitar, ARP synthesizer, harmonium, piano, Mellotron
Chris Judge Smith: percussion, backing vocals
Paul Whitehead: percussion
Produced at Trident Studios, December 1973 – April 1974 by Peter Hammill
UK release date and label: August 1974; Charisma. US release date and label: 1992, Caroline
Running time: 47:47

Hammill began to record his fourth solo album, *In Camera*, in December 1973, shortly before *Silent Corner* hit the stores. *In Camera* was a monumental departure for him; aside from drum overdubs on two tracks from Guy Evans and the loaning of an upright piano from Hugh Banton, the other former VdGG members were absent from the entire recording.

Self-reliance in instrumentation wasn't the only way in which this album was markedly different from what had come before. All but two of the songs on *In Camera* were written around the time of recording. Before this, the recording process consisted of committing to tape songs that had existed in some written form for at least a year prior.

Hammill's home studio, Sofa Sound, had progressed to such an extent that he was able to confidently record the backing tracks for the entire album – and these tracks consist of very complex compositions. Later, at Trident Studios, he added vocals and Evans's drums, overdubbing his own four-track recordings onto the studio's state of the art twenty-four track system – Hammill has remarked that the reactions of studio technicians present during these sessions ranged from bemusement to disbelief.

In Camera, itself, as a title, is a long way from wordy but vague album titles like *Chameleon in the Shadow of the Night* and *The Silent Corner and the Empty Stage*. With fewer words, the potential meanings compounded: it could refer, self-evidently, to photography, but also, if one looks to the Italian language, *camera* translates to a bedroom or private chamber, which is exactly what Hammill's Sofa Sound studio refers to – a room in an attic. Perhaps more precisely, the phrase *in camera*, in Latin applies here: 'in a private or secret session, not in public', or, 'in the privacy of a judge's chambers' – the latter was a situation more recently referred to as 'in chambers'.

It's incredible to imagine already following Hammill's career as 1973 rolled into 1974, and then having the opportunity to discover and get lost in both this album and *Silent Corner* in the space of a year! Where *Silent Corner* cast light, and shadow, on everything it touched, *In Camera* flourished in darkness.

'Ferret and Featherbird' (Hammill)

The opening track of *In Camera* is actually a song originally written in early 1969 for *The Aerosol Grey Machine*, and in fact, an early recorded version of the song appears on the alternate tracklist of *Aerosol* that Hammill released on his own label in 1997. The *In Camera* version is very different from its 1960s counterpart. An extended intro gradually fades into full volume, with swooping snippets of strummed acoustic guitars, plucked electric guitars, and runs of notes on a piano meshing together to at last form a musical structure as Hammill begins singing. The meaning of the title seems to be locked securely *in camera*, but the gist of the song is apparent: the separation from a loved one in a relationship is bemoaned – finally, it is acknowledged that the time and distance that holds the two apart also holds the love that is the basis of their relationship in stasis – rather than destroyed, it is preserved, but, ironically, rendered sterile.

(No More) The Sub-Mariner' (Hammill)

Time and again, in various publications, Peter Hammill has noted that his work both solo and with VdGG can be characterised as 'serious fun', challenging the assumption that the material is excessively doom-laden. Case in point; the lyrics to 'Sub-Mariner'. They're full of obscure references to pop culture, specifically Marvel Comics (as in the title, punning on the comic-book character Prince Namor, the Sub-Mariner), but also British athletes like Peter May and Hollywood actors such as Humphrey Bogart. Lost youth, and specifically the paradox that, in theory, choice-making is a skill that becomes more honed with age, while the number of choices that can be made decreases the older one becomes. Piano, synthesizers, and many backing vocal tracks give this track its dauntingly memorable gravitas.

'Tapeworm' (Hammill)

The second of the old songs included on *In Camera*, 'Tapeworm' was written in 1971. Stretching beyond the hard-rock limits previously marked by 'Rock and Role', this song is a harbinger of the anarchic noise that would partly define the next solo album. Playing electric guitar, piano, and bass with fury, Hammill is joined by Guy Evans on drums for this ferocious, satisfying tune. It's another one that deals, lyrically, with childhood – this time with the youthfully perverse tendency towards self-destruction. Oh, and an a cappella middle-section, with multi-tracked falsetto backing vocals, of course!

'Again' (Hammill)

A brief respite between the fierce rock of 'Tapeworm' and the heavy grandeur of 'Faint-Heart and the Sermon', 'Again' is a searching, sorrowful little song that features Hammill on vocals, guitar, and what is likely a harpsichord setting on the ARP synthesizer that was used heavily in the making of the album. The music is tightly wound and fast-paced, while the vocals alternate between keeping pace and languorously stretching out. 'Again' became a staple of Hammill's live set in future decades, and it was often performed as an encore, and sometimes, though less often, sung a cappella!

'Faint-Heart and the Sermon' (Hammill)
'Faint-Heart and the Sermon' is a mini-epic that would be picked up by the reformed VdGG on their tour the following year, along with 'A Louse Is Not a Home' and 'Forsaken Gardens' from the previous album. Awash in watery but forceful synths, and portentous lyrics filled with literary and religious references as well as awkward metaphors, 'Faint-Heart' can be seen as a sequel of sorts to 'The Lie'. While still questioning the nature of 'faith', Hammill turns his unwavering flashlight inward as well as outward, holding himself as accountable as he does the Church. The second song on the album to namecheck American culture ('Namor' and 'Humphrey Bogart' in 'Submariner' and the eponymous Herman Melville character 'Billy Budd' here), one might note that Hammill, in an interview from 2019, confessed to being a 'victim' of cryptic crosswords, and that 'American' is an anagram for 'In Camera'. When VdGG reformed in 1975, 'Faint-Heart' was a staple of their live performances.

'The Comet, the Course, the Tail' (Hammill)
This song features the Peter Hammill Guitar Quartet – all four parts (two electric, one acoustic, and one bass guitar) played by Hammill, of course. Another mini-epic, 'Comet' finds our singer making proclamations, at times almost archly, concerning the nature of free will and destiny, and to what extent our lives are shaped by both. The vocals, too, have considerable interplay; it is less of a case of one voice in the front and numerous backing vocals than it is a group of voices, carefully positioned in the sonic spectrum to be more or less equally audible. Sometimes all the voices combine their power in chorus, and other times they play off each other in supporting agreement or in counterpoint. 'Comet' was even more of a live fixture than 'Again' in Hammill's solo performances following the final breakup of VdGG. Its loose structure made it the perfect vehicle for two guitarists, or for guitar and violin, as well as for solo guitar, so it was often played in purely solo shows as well as in concerts that paired Hammill with violinists Graham Smith or Stuart Gordon, or with ex-Vibrators guitarist John Ellis as an opening for the four-piece K Group shows of the early 1980s.

'Gog' (Hammill)
'Magog (In Bromine Chambers)' (Hammill)
Where the previous two Hammill albums have closed with epic-length prog-rock tracks, *In Camera* presents its listeners with something entirely next-level. Prog is an insufficient descriptor for what goes on in 'Gog' and its companion piece, 'Magog'. The foreboding swirl of organ and synth, harmonium, thundering drums and unearthly vocals, achieves something

utterly otherworldly and primal.

Putting aside lyrical examinations of religious faith, free will versus destiny, and the potential moral pitfalls that increase with age, Hammill has gone back to the sci-fi leanings of 'Pioneers Over c', except here the lyrics are closer to dark fantasy (an unholy melding of C. S. Lewis with Arthur Machen) than anything else. It's daunting enough to contemplate the thinking of a god positioned according to our collective moral compasses, but to imagine a god, as Hammill has done here, with a concept of good and evil that is completely alien to our own is, at best, spine-chilling. VdGG would tackle this song in their live shows, to incredible effect – transcribing and arranging the musical madness that up until then only existed in Hammill's head. Serious fun, taken to the extreme.

On the original LP version of *In Camera*, there was never any break between 'Gog' and 'Magog', but one was always intended to exist, and this mistake was corrected with the 2006 remastered CD version. 'Magog' sounds like an instrumental soundtrack to a day in the life of a world where a god like the one described in the previous paragraph held court. It's post-apocalyptic musique concrete, performed by Hammill, Chris Judge Smith and Paul Whitehead on percussion, and Smith again on 'choral' vocals. About a minute into the track, Hammill gives a recitation of a lyric that reads like a short poem, with the recording slowed down to the point that the words become unintelligible – a problem easily solvable by increasing the RPM on one's turntable.

Following the bizarre incantation, the album closes out with more of the same gloriously creepy sounds – simple but demonic children's toys come to mind, as well as heavy machinery in the distance. There are plenty of sounds buried just under the mix, such as meditative breathing, that will reward repeated listenings, but at the same time, 'Magog' exists outside of any narrative that might supply a cohesive structure to *In Camera* – if not outside our plane of existence entirely.

Bonus Tracks
'The Emperor in His War-Room' (Hammill)
'Faint-Heart and the Sermon' (Hammill)
'(No More) the Sub-Mariner' (Hammill)
Surprisingly, the excellent version of 'Comet' that Hammill played at the 1978 gig in Kansas City was not used here, despite the addition of other songs from that performance on relevant reissued solo albums (see bonus tracks on *Chameleon in the Shadow of the Night* and *The Silent Corner and the Empty Stage*, above). The bonus tracks that were chosen, however, are stunning. All three are from the same John Peel Session, broadcast on BBC Radio 1 on 3 September, 1974. With majestic voice and minimal piano arrangement, Hammill brings the VdGG chestnut from four years earlier up to date with the two contemporary pieces, which actually benefit from the stripped-down attention to the skeletons of the songs.

Nadir's Big Chance (1975)

Personnel:

Hugh Banton: bass guitar, piano, Hammond organ

Guy Evans: drums and percussion

Peter Hammill: vocals, acoustic and electric guitars, bass, Hohner clavinet, piano

David Jackson: saxophone

Produced at Rockfield Studios and Trident Studios, December 1974, by Peter Hammill

UK release date and label: February 1975; Charisma. US release date and label: 1995; Caroline

Running time: 48:24

After the intensity of *In Camera*, no one could blame Hammill for wanting to swing in the opposite direction, away from all the intellectual investigations into religion and philosophy, and just have fun. But it's not that simple, of course. For all its seeming ponderousness, *In Camera* was also a blast – 'Tapeworm' begged for a loud car stereo and the open road, at least for prog fans, and 'Gog' was, among other things, an excursion into reckless abandon. So, although *Nadir's Big Chance* was certainly a departure from what came before, it's safe to say that its building blocks can be found in the chaos of the previous album.

It's also become a matter of common knowledge, among music fans, prog and otherwise, that *Nadir's Big Chance* was a revolutionary and ground-breaking album: it was among the chief catalysts for the upcoming wave of punk rock that would swell and crest a few years later. John 'Johnny Rotten' Lydon famously name-checked Hammill as a worthy combatant, while vilifying the rest of the progressive rock artists, calling their music bloated and irrelevant.

It's apparent that Hammill did have fun with this record, tongue-in-cheekily adopting a rebelliously teenage persona (or as the liner notes would have it, temporarily adopted by said persona) named Rikki Nadir – a critical wink, perhaps, at Ziggy Stardust or Freddie Mercury and the excesses that their personas signified. It was this anarchic and untamed portion of Hammill's psyche, then, that was responsible for the songs on *Nadir's Big Chance*.

The notoriety the album has garnered over the years as the reason the phrase 'godfather of punk' is so often adjacent to Hammill's name shouldn't obscure the fact that it's a highly successful album in its own way, standing head and shoulders with the previous year's two imposing releases. One coming to this album for the first time fresh from the pages of a *MOJO* special issue on the birth of punk might be surprised to learn that it's not overwhelmingly loud and aggressive from start to finish. Song for song, there are almost as many reflective, balladic numbers as there are fist-pumping anthems.

Despite the oil and water relationship that prog and punk had with each other, this album has closer ties with Van der Graaf Generator than either of the previous two solo albums. VdGG founding member Chris Judge Smith wrote one of the songs on the album and co-wrote another one with Hammill, and another song is a re-working of the first single VdGG released, pre-*Aerosol Grey Machine*. Perhaps the strongest tie the 'Nadir' album has to the band is that it, more than any solo album to date, heavily features the erstwhile VdGG members. Banton, Evans, and Jackson are, in fact, on every track! The band had decided to reform just before the recording of *Nadir's Big Chance*, and realised that making the album together would be a great way to catch up with each other musically and regain their footing as a band.

'Nadir's Big Chance' (Hammill)
Thundering bass and drums slightly precede Hammill/Nadir's no-quarter '1-2-3-4' count-in, and from there, all guitar, sax and hell break loose. The title track is a brief abstract of the album's thesis: that the music industry was in peril and the correct way forward was to play close to one's heart and not to trust the system. Perhaps overly simplistic and reductive for someone who, less than a year earlier, released an album with songs like 'Faint-heart and the Sermon' and 'Gog', but it's all part of the fun, too. A more lingering focus on the 'fun' part of the 'serious fun' equation; tackling serious matters, for sure, but with fist-pumps and head-nods more than discretion and precision. Behind the convenient 'Rikki' mask, it's still Hammill urging listeners to 'scratch the system with a song'.

'The Institute of Mental Health, Burning' (Hammill, Smith)
Guy Evans's strident drumming takes us out of the maelstrom of the opening track, and, without a break, into this song, originally a number written and performed by Hammill and Chris Judge Smith in the earliest days of VdGG, when they were just a duo. The song refers to a fire they witnessed on their university campus (also the impetus for 'w'!). Both Hammill and Banton play piano, backwards. A slight fable of a song that recalls late 1960s hits like the Carole King / Gerry Goffin-penned 'Pleasant Valley Sunday' or Scott Walker's 'Plastic Palace People', though the metaphors in 'Institute' are directed more at governmental authority than societal standards.

'Open Your Eyes' (Hammill)
This one has a little bit more of a groove than most Hammill/VdGG songs. Banton's keyboards pull from the soul sounds of the early 70s, and Jackson's sax-soloing towards the end brings a level of funkiness heretofore unheard from the 'wall of horns'. The Hammill/Nadir vocals stretch and soar rather huskily, as the lyrics evoke a place and time in his youth – where he was turned on to the power of live music for the first time: the chain of clubs known as the 'Locarnos' – which no longer exist.

'Nobody's Business' (Hammill)
This track starts off with a deeply sinister vibe and just expands on that as it progresses, as the listener goes from feeling as if he or she is in the airlock

of a spaceship cruising a Gog-controlled universe to free-floating in that universe. The heavily-feedbacked guitars whip around the sonic landscape, as do the extreme vocals, and it's all quite disorienting. The rhythm section and saxophone attack provide little in the way of grounding – it's all breathtakingly chaotic. If 'Slender Threads' was a mild reproach directed at a former compatriot who may have lost her way in the world of fashion modelling, 'Nobody's Business' is a much harsher and acerbic take on the same situation.

'Been Alone So Long' (Smith)
This is certainly what Hammill was referring to in the liner notes when he mentioned Nadir's penchant for 'weepy ballads' alongside 'the beefy punk songs' and 'the soul struts'. It's a beautifully-written study, by Chris Judge Smith, of self-doubt and insecurity in the context of a romantic relationship, and Jackson's sax playing is among his most successful accompaniments on any Hammill solo album; his sense of tone and phrasing could not have been more sympathetic to the subject and the song. The rest of the usual suspects are there, on guitar, drums, and bass, but Jackson steals the show.

'Pompeii' (Hammill)
Evans's drumming veers dangerously from the proto-punk aesthetic, with flourishes that threaten to reveal a prog flag hidden among the black leather. Lyrically, this is also the most atypical song on the album – it's not about a relationship, or the 'state of things' in any socio-political sense – it's a depiction of the lives of the inhabitants of Pompeii just prior to the volcanic disaster that killed them but preserved the city. Hard to derive anything 'punk' from this, but, on its own merits, it's a lovely song, and another one from the 'old days' of the late 1960s. Intricate and gentle playing among the quartet, but the song remains a contextual oddball.

'Shingle Song' (Hammill)
Another relatively placid tune that works well as a companion to 'Been Alone So Long', this one is also concerned with romance from the perspective of someone who's been left behind by their partner. Eschewing the interiority of Smith's lyrics to 'Been Alone So Long', Hammill finds metaphors and portents in the weather patterns occurring at the meeting of land and sea. The song slowly builds up a momentum and breaks into an unexpected, but beautifully fitting, instrumental, before returning to the main motif, and taking its leave as Hammill repeats the last two lines with a style reminiscent of Lou Reed – somehow the pain inherent in the situation is conveyed by the vocal equivalent of a glassy-eyed stare. Hammill sounds shell-shocked and subdued in the face of the sea's expanse, but not entirely cowed. 'I can't get you out of my mind / No, no, I just can't get you from my mind'. It's the presence in his mind of the one who's gone ahead that seems to be, ironically, sparking his will to keep going.

'Airport' (Hammill)

Electric guitars and power chords are back, but this song is poppier than the title track or 'Nobody's Business'. It's similar, in a sense, to the previous track, but rather than the partner having already gone ahead, they're leaving, now, in the time-frame of the song as sung. So, the vocals veer between the heightened angst of the singer seeing his loved one depart and not being able to do anything about it, and coming to terms with the fact that they're, for all intents and purposes, gone, even though still in view. The airport/airplane motif works well for establishing this kind of dynamic, and the band does a good job at mirroring the fluctuating senses of panic and resignation by laying down a propulsive rhythm, suggesting a clear trajectory, while alternating between melodies that are insistent and mournful, depending on whether the singer is in longing or resolute mode. It's also comparatively brash and youthful-sounding. You get the sense that this is the sorrow of a lad who will be thinking about the next girl in five or ten minutes.

'People You Were Going To' (Hammill)

This is a bonafide remake of a VdGG song! It first appeared as a single and then a track on *The Aerosol Grey Machine*. It aged well in the intervening six years, and the musicians do well by it. Hammill sings it in a lower register than usual, and the rest of the band play it at a significantly slower tempo than VdGG did on the original recording. Once again, David Jackson's sax provides extraordinarily strong glue, holding everything in place and letting it swing from the last chorus to the mutated call and response version of the chorus that closes out the song, with Banton, Jackson, and Evans providing counter-harmonies.

'Birthday Special' (Hammill)

Hammill regards this one as the definitive punk song, in a musical sense, in the 'Nadir' collection, noting the prominence of the 'three-chord trick' that so much of the punk movement was built on. The lyrics are surprisingly silly, but as Hammill also noted, any subject matter that veered close to VdGG territory had to be avoided for this album, because a reunion and subsequent album had already been decided on. In any case, this song is a lot of fun, with a gigantic rave-up for an intro, a couple of verses and choruses that the band barely settle down for, an instrumental break, another rave-up, and then done and out. This was also released as a 7" single by Charisma, with 'Shingle Song' as its B-side, on 24 January 1975.

'Two or Three Spectres' (Hammill)

Rikki Nadir leaves us with a groove and a prophecy. Both have held up over time. Sinewy bass lines (played here by Hammill himself – his first time writing a song on the instrument) weave in and around Jackson's short, punctuated bursts of sax, and Evans and Banton fill in the rest of the scene with drums and keyboards. It all does sound a little like Stevie Wonder – close listeners will hear, at the very beginning of the track, a call which sounds like, 'Oh, why didn't you say? You want more Stevie Wonder!'

The band barely manage to establish the aforementioned groove before Hammill/Nadir is off on a tear, ranting and excoriating the music industry heads for their abuse of musicians, members of the music press for their attention to all the wrong details, the fashionable hangers-on for subverting any sense of artistic integrity, and even the arena-concert attending throngs of music fans – Hammill/Nadir, seeing the arena-mob-audiences at the start of the trend to book rock shows at enormous outdoor sports arenas, was uncomfortably reminded of pictures of Nazi rallies: 'Ten thousand peace signs mark the entry of the sax. / Ten thousand peace signs / but they're different from the back'.

Godbluff (1975)

Personnel:
Hugh Banton: organ, bass
Guy Evans: drums, percussion
Peter Hammill: vocals, piano, guitar
David Jackson: saxophone, flute
Produced at Rockfield Studios, June 1975 by Van der Graaf Generator
UK release date and label: October 1975; Charisma. US release date and label:
1976; Mercury
Running time: 37:44

While *Nadir's Big Chance* was being rehearsed and recorded, the decision to reform the band was a well-kept secret. When the four-piece was satisfied with the new passel of songs they'd written, they announced that there would be a tour and an album later in 1975. *Godbluff*, in fact, was released in October of that year, after a concentrated burst of touring to whet people's appetites and pique their collective interest. The new album was recorded at Rockfield Studios, as was *Nadir's Big Chance* before it, and the band had more than enough material. In fact, the entirety of the next album, *Still Life,* was already written, as was the song 'Masks', which would appear on the third of three albums VdGG would release before the end of 1976, *World Record*!

Although the band had recorded six of their new songs in the *Godbluff* sessions (the four album tracks, plus 'Pilgrims' and 'La Rossa'), Guy Evans claims responsibility for the brainstorm that led to making the new record so compact and brief, with four songs clocking in at approximately 38 minutes. Evans remembers being alone with the song titles on pieces of paper, shuffling them around, and realizing that 'Undercover Man', 'Scorched Earth', 'Arrow', and 'Sleepwalkers' fit together in a way that seemed to make perfect sense as an album, even if it wasn't possible to articulate exactly what held those four together.

Evans went on to say that *Godbluff* was among his favourite VdGG albums because of its live feel. The band didn't have to resort to a lot of studio work to record the songs the way they thought they should sound – it was very easy to tap into whatever force it was that made them Van der Graaf Generator. That ease, Evans remarked, was missing in the *Still Life* recording sessions.

One of the main differences between the VdGG that split in 1972 and the new iteration was Hammill's new-found fascination with, if not necessarily mastery of, the electric guitar. It made for a much more modern and direct sound and alternately meshed with and challenged Jackson's highly electric sax arsenal.

'The Undercover Man' (Hammill)

This was the only one of the four *Godbluff* songs that wasn't written prior to the VdGG reunion rehearsals. An instant audience favourite during the 1975-76 tours, the band would often open their concerts with it: Jackson's quietly pulsing flute accompanied Hammill's whispered vocals on stage as it did on the record when the needle dropped.

Hammill's enigmatic lyrics are sung first in a whisper, and then for the next minute or so the delivery remains sotto voce. Finally, the drums join in alongside the organ and flute interplay, and with that, the vocals kick in full-throttle. An instrumental break follows, with Hammill's new instrument, the Hohner Clavinet, facing off against Banton's established keyboard setup. The lyrics, still enigmatic, have moved on from what seems a self-reprisal at the mirror to an optimistically existential stock-taking: 'Even now, we are not lost'. There is an indication that the despair voiced in 'Lemmings' is being revisited and reimagined as opportunity. Likewise, the song, which started so tentatively, is gloriously launched into the upper atmosphere by some truly inspired playing from the band. There's a sense of uninterrupted forward thrust introduced in this song that would characterise the band's output from this point on.

'Scorched Earth' (Hammill, Jackson)

Although written well before 'The Undercover Man', 'Scorched Earth' seems of a piece with the previous track – the band flow from the closing notes of one into the introduction to the other. The forward thrust is maintained; although the song has a few different parts to it, they're not arrived at in a meandering fashion. Rather, the sections are all points on a line that informs the song.

In any case, the band play with a galvanising fury, echoing Hammill's militaristic lyrical metaphors. Almost as soon as they get going, however, the band hits foggy ground. Back to zero, tentatively kicking in again as the new territory is being examined, the music quickly makes the hallucinatory confusion of the atmosphere its own, laying down an appropriate backdrop for Hammill's outraged but confounded lyrics, delivered with a precision that is oxymoronically crystal clear and hallucinatory, thanks to the mastery of backing vocal overdubs.

With that, it's a return to the theme established at the outset, but this, again, quickly gives way to one of VdGG's most ferocious instrumental onslaughts that ends with a majestic reprise of the theme, and a deliciously perverse slice of abrasive guitar feedback.

'Arrow' (Hammill)

Side Two opens with an anomaly in the VdGG canon (up to this point). Free improvisation! Evans seems to be the ringleader here, with Banton and Jackson tentatively adding bass and sax, respectively. In fact, the free-playing was not planned, but rather done on the spur of the moment by Evans, who had become irritated by a long succession of attempts to record the intro – he wanted to change it up, and his variation was kept for the record.

Eventually, the song's melody materialises, and with Hammill's severe (even for him) vocal delivery, crystallises into a fearsome vehicle to behold. Continuing the lyrical theme of time as an elemental force to be reckoned with,

Above: Signs of the times: (L to R) Hammill, Jackson, Banton and Evans, pawning their hearts in 1971.

Below: And then there were two… pints. VdGG band meeting, 2016.

Left: *The Aerosol Grey Machine.* The album that started it all, featuring bassist Keith Ellis, who left VdGG afterwards to join Juicy Lucy, and later, Boxer. *(Mercury)*

Right: *The Least We Can Do Is Wave To Each Other.* David Jackson's and Nic Potter's first album with VdGG, and the first of the band's two releases in 1970. *(Charisma)*

Left: The US version of *H to He* had a very different look from the UK version, but both featured the painting 'Birthday' by Paul Whitehead. *(Charisma)*

Right: Peter Hammill's first solo album featured the piano from Elton John's 'Candle in the Wind' and the mandolinist who played on Rod Stewart's 'Maggie May.' *(Charisma)*

Left: According to Hugh Banton, the title came about due to the band mishearing David Jackson when he uttered the phrase 'horn parts.' *(Charisma)*

Right: 'Chameleon' marks the first appearance of Hammill's ubiquitous monogram which includes the letters of his surname and the Scorpio sign. *(Charisma)*

Left: *The Silent Corner And The Empty Stage*. 'Wilhelmina,' from this album, was written for Guy Evans's new-born daughter. *(Charisma)*

Right: *In Camera* was only one of two instances in which cover artist Paul Whitehead was credited with playing an instrument. *(Charisma)*

Left: *Nadir's Big Chance*. The cover photographs were credited to one Dino M'brela, one of the many pseudonyms coined by Hammill over the years! *(Charisma)*

Right: *Godbluff*. The Escher-esque VDGG logo first appeared here. It was designed by John Pasche, who also created the iconic Rolling Stones 'lips' logo. *(Charisma)*

Left: *Still Life*. The cover art represents the actual image of a spark produced by a Van de Graaff Generator. *(Charisma)*

Right: *World Record*. The only VdGG album to get an Argentinian release, where it bore the title Record Mundial. *(Charisma)*

Left: *The Quiet Zone / The Pleasure Dome.* The inner sleeve portrait of the band was one of the first album photographs credited to Anton Corbijn. *(Charisma)*

Right: *Vital.* The only album to feature late addition to the band Charles Dickie. *(Charisma)*

Left: The undercover man: Hammill performing the *Godbluff* album with VdGG, Belgium, 1975.

Right: Van der Graaf violinist and Hammill musical foil, Graham Smith is caught here slightly after VdG came to an end.

Below: The late VdGG bassist Nic Potter, being interviewed in 2009.

Right: A stop on the 1979 Peter Hammill/Graham Smith US tour. Crimson royalty in attendance!

Hammill Travels To N.Y.

Gathered backstage at the Bottom Line in New York following Charisma artist Peter Hammill's recent performance are (front row, l-r): Graham Smith, group member; Robert Fripp, Gail Colson, Hit and Run Management; Peter Hammill; Bob Barnes, Charisma; Mike Farrell, William Morris Agency; and Nancy Lewis, GM, Charisma; (back row, l-r): Walter O'Brien, Run It Music; Fred Weissman; Jim Del Belzo; and Don Bernstine, Polydor (Charisma's U.S. distributor).

This page:
The only time
(in the 1970s)
that 'A Plague
of Lighthouse
Keepers' was
performed live
was in a television
studio in Belgium,
March 1972.

Hugh Banton...

David Jackson...

...and Peter
Hammill (toasting
his bandmates
and the audience
during the
'Plague' finale).

This page:
Guy Evans, David Jackson, and Hugh Banton performing the *Godbluff* album for Belgian TV in Charleroi, 1975.

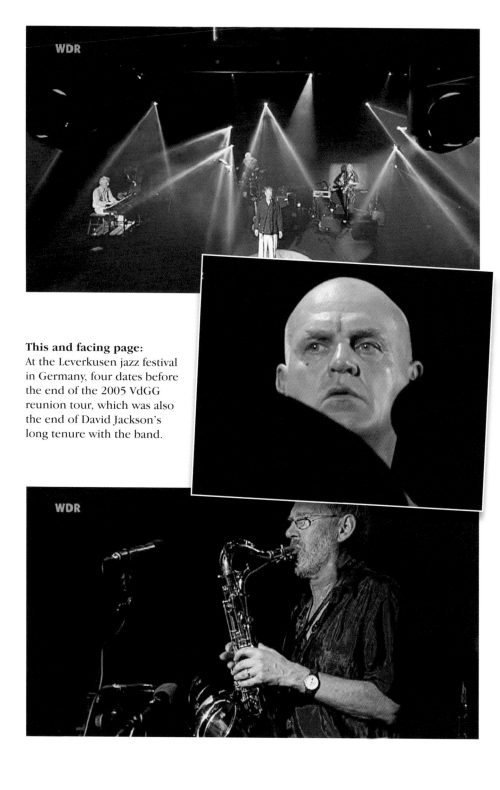

This and facing page:
At the Leverkusen jazz festival in Germany, four dates before the end of the 2005 VdGG reunion tour, which was also the end of David Jackson's long tenure with the band.

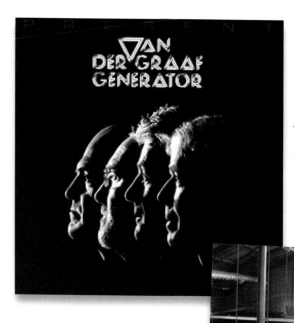

Left: VdGG, profiled! Evans, Jackson, Hammill, and Banton line up for the cover photo of *Present,* their 2005 reunion album. *(Esoteric)*

Right: VdGG's first album as a trio, attempting to find the square of the hypotenuse with *Trisector* (2008). *(Esoteric)*

Left: The trend towards math-rock continues (in the titles, anyway) with 2011's *A Grounding in Numbers. (Esoteric)*

Right: A latter-day *Time Vaults* – VdGG push experimentation to extremes with *ALT*. *(Esoteric)*

Left: The final time, to date, that VdGG disturbed a studio – 2016's *Do Not Disturb*. *(Esoteric)*

Right: *Time Vaults*. VdGG's 'odds and sods' from the 'lost' 1970s period. An 'anti-compilation', according to Hammill. *(Sofa Sound)*

Above & below: The 21st Century VdGG trio play at a small venue in London, in December 2010, several months prior to the release of *A Grounding in Numbers*.

Above: The trio in Berlin, 2013, perhaps playing the tour's centrepiece, 'A Plague of Lighthouse Keepers'!

Below: Peter Hammill performing solo in 2019 – a rendition of the VdGG classic, 'Still Life'.

Above & below: Pioneers, refugees, and pilgrims: Banton, Hammill, Evans, at work and at rest.

and a philosophical conundrum to come to terms with, 'Arrow' gets to the heart of humanity's inability to reconcile its perception of time with the fact of time's absolute and unconditionally final word.

As in 'Scorched Earth', the band plays on well past the end of Hammill's lyric, showcasing, again, the incongruous sound of Hammill's Hohner clavinet, as well as the rare occasion of Banton playing bass.

'The Sleepwalkers' (Hammill)

'The Sleepwalkers' is as close as VdGG get to a 'prog epic' on *Godbluff*. Stretching slightly over ten minutes, and with two distinct sections, one might be forgiven for thinking that they've gone back into *Pawn Hearts* territory. Evans's ominous drum beat and Banton's strident keyboard work, which open 'The Sleepwalkers' with a jolt, deftly put such thoughts to rest. The song starts as an exploration of the dream-state from within; Hammill's lyrics are from the point of view of one sleepwalker among many, although the metaphor seems to shift from one of actual sleeping/dreaming to the philosophical critique of humanity as sleepwalkers, asleep even while awake. Nevertheless, time is invoked again, in the sense that there is not enough of it to explore what the dreaming world has to offer, or perhaps not enough time to discover the secrets in our own minds.

In an abrupt break in the first section, thanks to Banton's twisted sense of humour, the band breaks into a sinister but tongue-in-cheek cha-cha, before returning to the thundering riff already laid down. There follows a brief reprise of the established theme, which flows into a shimmering soundscape primarily made up of cascades of cymbals and organ chords. The listener comes out of the other end of this reverie into the second part of the song; a seemingly less complex musical structure that hews more closely to a rock motif. Hammill briefly switches lyrical tacks and becomes something of an interlocutor, addressing the listener, before slipping back into the role of a hapless sleepwalker. The lyric in its entirety is a thrilling and fascinating meditation on the world of sleep, and what to make of the dichotomy, both direct and metaphorical, of the division of time between sleep and wakefulness. And, of course, the nagging question: are we ever truly awake?

'The Sleepwalkers' is an exhilarating composition with which to end VdGG's reunion album. The songwriting and playing show a band fully able to realise their potential and deliver a song that takes the best of their previously ultra-complex song structures and arranges them in a way that fits the streamlined propulsion that characterises the reformed band without forfeiting the essence of what originally made them so unique.

The remastered edition of *Godbluff* that was released in 2005 contains two bonus tracks. Both are live VdGG performances from L'Altro Mondo in Rimini, Italy, on 9 August 1975, on the tour leading up to the album's initial release. The renditions of 'A Louse Is Not a Home' and 'Forsaken Gardens' are vintage VdGG in terms of execution, but the recording quality suffers.

Still Life (1976)

Personnel:
Hugh Banton: organ, bass pedals, bass guitar, Mellotron, piano
Guy Evans: drums and percussion
Peter Hammill: vocals, guitar, piano
David Jackson: alto, tenor, and soprano saxophones, and flute
Produced at Rockfield Studios, June 1975 and January 1976 by Van der Graaf
Generator
UK release date and label: April 1976; Charisma. US release date and label: 1976;
Mercury.
Running time: 44:57

Firmly back in the music world with a positive critical review of *Godbluff*,
VdGG were 'charging madly forward', as the lyric for 'Scorched Earth' has it,
and released *Still Life*, the second of three post-reunion albums, and the first of
two for 1976.

Despite the success of *Godbluff* and the warm reception the band received
in live venues, they were finding it difficult to cope as a band – health issues
had overtaken Banton, and VdGG were the victims of politically motivated
harassment in Italy, having their gear stolen and held for ransom, and being
threatened with violence at concert venues. So, they were understandably
relieved to be done with that particular spate of touring and to be able to get
back into recording mode. Some of their work was already done: 'Pilgrims' and
'La Rossa' had already been recorded during the 'Godbluff' sessions.

For his part, Evans was significantly less excited about the *Still Life* sessions
than those for *Godbluff*. He felt there wasn't the same spirit of 'VdGG-ness' that
seemed to appear out of nowhere for the previous session. They had to work at
achieving the same level of the elusive, 'you know it when you have it' quality,
which, according to Evans, meant abandoning the very spirit of VdGG. Dismayed
and detached, he felt that they had reached this level during the recording of
Godbluff and in live performance, but didn't feel that the band was remotely
close to that state during the recording of *Still Life*, and it left him frustrated. The
other members were rather more positive in their assessments of the making of
the album and the quality of the songs, which we will see presently.

'Pilgrims' (Hammill, Jackson)

One of the tracks recorded during the *Godbluff* sessions, 'Pilgrims' is an
uncharacteristically bright-eyed, optimistic song for VdGG. With lyrics
reminiscent of 'Refugees', but backed by an altogether less mournful
composition, the band opened *Still Life* with a tune that, at its climax,
verges on the ecstatic. The lyrical 'I' turns to 'we' as a sort of rejection to the
loneliness that marks the point of entry into the song. 'Pilgrims' can also be
seen as a sequel to the final track on *Godbluff*, 'Sleepwalkers': 'I rise from
lifelong sleep. // It seems such a long time I've dreamed – / now, awake, I can

see / we are pilgrims and so must walk this road…'

Banton's organ intro foreshadows the optimistic brightness as the track begins, even if the lyrics and the song proper take a while to catch up. The band soars through two longish verses with corresponding choruses, before Hammill's declaration of victory – 'All of us, Pilgrims!' – cues a fanfare that in turn whips the music (this section written by Jackson) into the territory of fist-pumping and heightened emotionality.

'Still Life' (Hammill)

Despite, or perhaps, perversely, because of, the high note listeners were left with at the close of 'Pilgrims', the next track is the brooding, dark 'Still Life'. The title track is built around an extended monologue sung by Hammill and accompanied, majestically and not a little spookily, by Banton on organ. Just before the three-minute mark, the full force of VdGG is counted in for a vicious repudiation of immortality – a state which, in a nod to sci-fi, Hammill's narrator had been bemoaning. The pace eventually slows as Hammill's vocal tirade winds down, and, his piano supplanting the organ, he sombrely finishes his argument for living a life and being able to die. The band come back for a finale, majestic but subdued.

'La Rossa' (Hammill)

The third track on *Still Life* probably wins the prize for the VdGG song that most brazenly rocks out. In the ensuing ten minutes, the band seem to forget (if they ever truly believed) they were a progressive rock band. Playing with what feels like near-reckless abandon, with Hammill out in front on electric guitar, 'La Rossa' sees VdGG fully enjoying themselves and playing off each other. This is one of the earlier tracks recorded during the *Godbluff* sessions, and you can hear what Evans was getting at in his criticism of *Still Life* – while all the songs see VdGG at the top of their game, none of the other ones sound quite as gloriously full of life as 'La Rossa'.

As lengthy as the song is, originally plans were in place for it to be even longer. There was to be a reprise following the considerable build-up of the climax, where the song's protagonist finds he's been rebuffed by the woman he's been addressing. Thankfully, this section was cut and eventually ended up in 'Lost and Found' on Hammill's *Over* album.

'My Room (Waiting for Wonderland)' (Hammill)

'My Room' was quite a departure for the band. A quiet song, but not in the same way as previous 'quiet' VdGG songs like 'House with No Door' or 'Refugees', which were very busy despite being mellow. By contrast, 'My Room' features very minimal instrumental input from the band members – Hammill on piano and vocals, Banton on bass, Evans drumming, of course, and Jackson on sax. The performances from all the musicians are astounding in their sensitivity and depth – this is one place where the commonly thrown about canard of musicians being telepathic actually seems correct.

Banton's bass playing is extraordinarily sympathetic to the song, especially given that it's not his main instrument. Towards the end of 'My Room' the bass really stands out in the front of the mix, pushing the music forward while at the same time reining it in. It's Jackson, however, who really steals the show, with particularly doleful and haunting sax that grapples and parries with Hammill's piano and the rhythm section. He also provides some atmospheric textures in the background that really come through in the 2005 remastering of the album. Perhaps most remarkably, Hammill's vocals are singular in this instance. No backing vocal tracks, no overdubs. Just the one voice, which here is more than enough.

'Childlike Faith in Childhood's End' (Hammill)

VdGG finish off *Still Life* with a throwback to the 'epic' prog workouts of their earlier incarnation. 'Childlike Faith' has several themes and progresses through them all, but with more grace and finesse than the psychotic stop/start approach used in earlier compositions like 'Lost'. One abrupt change does occur at 7'35 – an introduction of two themes written by Banton and Jackson, respectively. The band hops from one to the other, and eventually the two merge before shifting back into the melody that carried the vocal prior to the break.

The band is out in full force on this tune – Jackson with flute and saxophones and Banton with organ and bass pedals. And of course, Hammill brings his A-game, outdoing himself on vocals, and supplying seemingly countless backing vocal tracks to boot. The band still had one more record and the better part of a year to go before calling it quits again, but this song would have been a fitting sign-off. Wilfully unfashionable as ever, they pulled out all the stops while Hammill delivered a lyric that looked at humanity's place in the grand scheme, wondering what comes next after humanity's inevitable termination (brazenly and courageously believing that something indeed will), and defiantly casting his lot with that unknowable 'levelling up', the band pay tribute to the ultimate life force. And, of course, Arthur C. Clarke.

Bonus Tracks
'Gog' (Hammill)

The 2005 remastered re-release of 'Still Life' contained one bonus track: a live version of 'Gog', performed at the Theatre Gwynedd, in Bangor, Wales on 10 May 1975. As with the bonus live tracks on the 'Godbluff' reissue, this is far from a stellar recording, but the performance is incredible. A definite high point of the band's mercurial live shows.

World Record (1976)

Personnel:
Hugh Banton: organ
Guy Evans: drums, percussion, cymbal
Peter Hammill: vocals, guitar, piano
David Jackson: saxophone, flute
Produced at Rockfield Studios, May 1976 by Van der Graaf Generator
UK release date and label: October 1976; Charisma. US release date and label:
1976, Mercury.
Running time: 52:19

For their second release in 1976 and the third in a two-year span, VdGG
opted for a more rock-oriented album, less steeped in the freak zone than
their previous efforts. Only to an extent, of course – they *were* Van der Graaf
Generator, after all. So *World Record* (the title perhaps a nod towards the
attempt at producing music that carried the VdGG stamp while existing for
all, instead of the elite few that the band was often criticised for catering to –
'VdGG is for everyone!' read a promotional sticker of the time) hit turntables
with five tracks, like *Still Life* before it, but the music was quite a bit more
down and dirty, and the lyrical concerns were earthier as well. Psychodrama
and uncomplicated (relatively!) spiritual longing took the place of sci-fi epics
of immortality and evolution; the examination of romantic/sexual relationships
was decidedly more straightforward. And, not least, the band experimented
with reggae! Hammill has noted that the personal trauma that he explored on
the solo album following this one, *Over*, was also interrogated in some of the
lyrical material on *World Record*.

'When She Comes' (Hammill)
The album leads off with a muscular, near-anthemic song that takes some
odd turns in its middle section. Evans leads the beast into a dusty side-alley,
and things get momentarily quieter – the bray and snort of the organ gives
way to carefully controlled swathes of feedback and Jackson switches from
sonic sax onslaught to breathy atmospherics. This more tentative approach
can't last, of course. Evans hastens the tempo and spurs the band back into
familiar realms of chaos and squall. Throughout, his drumming is tight and
relentless, and Jackson's sax attack is forceful and commanding. Banton's
organ contributions range from the established VdGG organ sound to effects
that are not as celestial-sounding as in previous efforts, but more terrestrially
vibrant. Hammill's grumpy-sounding electric guitar strums add peculiar but
perfect counterpoint. His vocals here are as raw, and as controlled, as ever –
listening to his vocal heroics, your own vocal cords may feel sympathetically
strained – and the judicious use of multi-tracking was never more effective,
especially in the delivery of the closing lines.
    Hammill's lyrics are more direct than usual, exploring the psychic and

karmic cost extracted from giving oneself over to 'la belle dame sans merci' (referencing the eponymous ballad written by Keats). The titular 'she' is also referred to in the song as 'the lady with her skin so white' and likened first to 'something out of Blake or Burne-Jones,' alluding to Keats' contemporaries in the poetic and visual arts, and then to Edgar Allan Poe. By deliberately comparing the visage of the 'lady' first to the work of artists who generally portray beauty in a positive manner, and then to the horrific, deathly images associated with Poe, Hammill is performing his own literary Poe-trick, allowing the lady to be revealed as a creature who, rather than emitting a pure white light, gives off a sicklier, pale glow while keeping the observer in a deathlike darkness. But, is it the fault of the lady, or does the person being addressed in the song do it to themselves, by disregarding all warning signs in a reckless bid for the lady's hand, regardless of the cost? There are echoes here of the bargain and cost mentioned in the song 'Still Life,' but here, the conceit is much more visceral and immediate, and feels far more dangerous.

An odd sense of danger, in fact, permeates this song. In embracing a more accessible approach, VdGG is, paradoxically, not playing to their strengths. But it is in pushing themselves to their limits, even if this situation is not what most bands would find limiting, that they shine most brightly.

'A Place to Survive' (Hammill)

Melding a very straight-ahead rock motif with some seriously demented envelope-pushing noise, VdGG seem to be laying down a late-period manifesto. Though the lyric exhorts the listener to 'stand straight,' come what may, it's tempting to read this song as a sort of 'note to self' for the band: they've done what they can in terms of connecting with a largely indifferent world, and all that's left is to keep going in the face of that indifference.

Hammill's vocal attack (and it really is an attack) animates the lyric, which is a maelstrom of popular self-help literature, reveille, and existentialism. It's delivered atop a series of riffs that the band bashes out with an infectiously joyful abandon. The verse-chorus-verse portion of the song ends just prior to the six-minute mark, and the remainder of the designated ten minutes plays out in an increasingly deranged recycling of the major riffs, during which each band member plays in an ever more wigged-out fashion: Banton's bass pedal attack is particularly manic, and Hammill's guitar sounds like it's being piped in from one of the deepest circles of Hades. It's VdGG at their most brutally joyous, life-affirming, noisiest best, keeping up a manic intensity that makes the climax of 'A Plague of Lighthouse Keepers' seem staid in comparison.

'Masks' (Hammill)

'Masks' was one of the songs written in the autumn of 1974, just prior to the *Godbluff* rehearsals. A sombre intro, led by mournful emoting from Jackson, seems welcome after the cacophony that closes out the previous track, but it's short-lived. Hammill's guitar is thrust into the foreground, competing with

Jackson's jittery sax stabs, while Banton's organ percolates and swirls just below the surface. The vocal delivery, with its use of short phrases and internal rhymes, feels very mannered, and in fact, the song itself is a study in restraint – when the song pauses at the three-minute mark, and again at 3:50, one would expect a release, but instead, with each dramatic change comes an increased level of tension. Finally, the only relief given to the listener is a return to the relatively calmer state that was experienced at the outset of the song, but that quickly ramps up to a fever pitch as the song nears its climax, and it abruptly ends unexpectedly, with the listener expecting a bit more of a resolution. The effect is akin to running up a flight of unfinished stairs and stopping an instant before the sudden drop.

Delving into Italian culture from the seventeenth century, Hammill invokes the sad clown character Pierrot to illustrate the psychological abuse that the subject of the lyric visits on himself as he alienates the people in his life. There is an interesting similarity between the accentuated pallor that is a trademark of Pierrot and the deathly white skin of the 'lady' in the album's opening track. Ultimately, though, Pierrot is just one of many masks worn by our antihero in this cautionary tale, and, given the self-castigating nature of some of the lyrics in the contemporaneous solo albums *Over* and *The Future Now*, one wonders whether 'Masks' isn't more of a fear of the lyricist losing his identity to the personae he puts into his songs than a 'past-tense' story of a nameless third-person character. Interestingly, 'Masks' was released as a 7" single by Charisma in France only, with the song divided into two parts over the record's A and B sides.

'Meurglys III, the Songwriter's Guild' (Hammill)

This is the band's latter-day 'Plague of Lighthouse-Keepers' in terms of length if not style. Eschewing the studio trickery used to create that ten-part suite, 'Meurglys III' (the name Hammill gave to the guitar used on this album), is differently epic. There are only a few times in which the structure of the song morphs significantly within the almost 21-minute running time. Hammill's singing parts are sparse throughout the track – four brief segments, three of which are completed by the song's halfway mark.

Hugh Banton begins 'Meurglys' with a mournful theme on the organ. After Banton plays through it once, David Jackson enters, playing the same melody on saxophone in a higher octave. On the third go around, Guy Evans joins in on drums, and the mournfulness gives way to a quirky sense of mischief as Jackson and Banton start adding a complexity to the proceedings, weaving lines of melody around each other. This goes on for just over a minute, at which point Hammill crashes in on guitar and adds a bit of drive and menace to the tune.

The song lopes forward from here, propelled by Banton, Jackson, and Evans, and guided by Hammill's guitar and vocals. This is mainly where the aforementioned 'personal trauma' comes into play in the lyrics. While much of

Hammill's approach on the songs on *Over* is confrontational – either towards the self or others – 'Meurglys' begins by way of explaining the current fragile state of the narrator (it's harder here to fully separate the writer from the lyrical protagonist since the latter self-identifies as a writer and guitarist) as he describes the terms and conditions of his self-imposed exile: 'These days I mainly just talk to plants and dogs / All human contact seems painful, risky, odd', and 'I find me gone from all but secret languages'. The four musicians barrel on to the four-minute mark, Hammill playing fewer notes but letting the guitar mirror the despair fuelled by the words, while Banton and Jackson respond to the guitar lines with frantic volleys of notes, the former with sympathetic organ chords as well as wonky and discordant piano work, ratcheting up the level of angst that's perhaps both the cause and effect of the meaning behind the sung text.

Here, the band pulls back and starts anew, as Hammill begins the second part of the lyric, expounding further on his situation. This section begins and remains comparatively laid back, and there's a lot of space between the notes and the instruments. It feels very cautiously intuitive: each musician skitters around the others with what seems like a sense of reverence. Eventually, the sense of relying on intuition begins to recede, and a theme begins to coalesce. Banton and Hammill in particular start to assert themselves with more emphatic playing, and eventually come to a head before veering into something different just after the eight-minute mark.

It's not vastly different from what was played before – there's still the laconic and expressive lead guitar lines followed by the barrage of notes played by Jackson and Banton to bring the band up to the beginning of the next measure. Before long, though, Hammill fills in on both the front and back end with guitar, and the horns and keyboards come closer to centre stage in the lead-in parts as well. This goes on for a full minute before Hammill re-enters the fray with his third set of lyrics. The vocals here are recorded differently – they sound rougher and more compressed, and, as is often the case, there are multi-tracked Hammill backing vocals. Here, he's switched to a declamatory second-person approach, for what at first sounds like a metaphysical pep talk, before morphing (devolving?) into derision and reproach, echoing the complaint made at the beginning of the song with masterful rhetorical skill: 'When no more plants or dogs or rooms are there to hear you / And no one is left near you, then you'll see / In the end, there's only you and Meurglys III / And this is just what you chose to be / Fool!' Following the end of Hammill's diatribe, the band extend this movement a bit further before changing direction again.

Veering off toward distant prog outposts, the band storms through a brief and intricate passage. Every instrument interlocks with each other, even the guitar, for once cooperating instead of providing counterpoint. As the band finally combusts, mostly spontaneously, Hammill emerges alone with his guitar, singing and playing a soft, bluesy refrain that closes out the lyrical narration. The conclusion is as ambiguous as the final sung part of 'A Plague of Lighthouse-Keepers': all we know is that the narrator intends to keep going despite the internal and external pressures causing and prolonging the trauma. But VdGG is far from done with 'Meurglys'.

As Hammill finishes singing, the band kick back in, this time with Jackson and Hammill trading licks back and forth over the surprisingly appropriate reggae backdrop produced by Evans's drumming and Banton's bass pedals and mostly staccato organ playing. And this is how 'Meurglys' eventually finishes, with the last seven minutes spent in an otherworldly zone somewhere between reggae and prog rock. With a few minutes to spare, Hammill and Jackson turn the laid-back vibe on its head with a fiercely scathing joint rave-up. In a disarmingly bizarre fashion, very different, again, from the 'Plague' finale, they've illustrated in musical terms the ambiguity presented by the lyrics.

'Wondering' (Banton, Hammill)

The final song on the final VdGG album of the seventies proved to be the ideal wrap-up. It's a stately composition that is at once restrained and exuberant, sombre and celebratory. Banton's multi-layered organ parts, some incisive, others dreamy, do the bulk of the work here; aside from an introductory duet between Banton and Jackson that's somewhat reminiscent of the beginning of 'The Undercover Man', Jackson's horn playing, Evans's drumming, and Hammill's piano all play a minor role.

Hammill's voice is as clear and upfront as it's ever been in a Van der Graaf recording. Every nuance, tic and shade are thrown into sharp aural relief. The lyrics depict a person who seems to have reached the end of a journey, knowing, or discovering, that it's just the finale of a segment of a longer one. It's an emotional tour de force and provides a sense of relief following the nightmarish claustrophobia of much of the previous track. Once again, the lyrics reach an ambiguous non-closure, but this time, the sense of resignation is replaced by ecstatic anticipation: 'This ridiculous brain / Now bursts with joy!' As the band – again, mainly Banton – riff over the melody, Hammill repeats the refrain, 'Wondering if it's all been true', which is a concise and apt summation of the almost ten-year VdGG history.

Although it is understood that all members of the band have a hand in shaping the final form of the songs, they're usually credited to Hammill as the writer who has brought them to the band in a form sufficiently complete to allow for tinkering and arranging. 'Wondering', however, is credited to Banton and Hammill. As Banton remembers, he'd sent Hammill a tape of instrumental music, well before the writing and recording of *World Record* took place. It wasn't Banton's own music; he likely sent it to Hammill to illustrate a point regarding style, but when Hammill came back to it after a period of time, he misidentified it as a piece that Banton had written, and began to write lyrics for it, which became 'Wondering'. When Hammill then delivered the song, such as it was, back to Banton, he realised he was going to have to write a new tune to go with the lyrics that Hammill had written for someone else's music, and that was how the 'Wondering' that appeared on 'World Record' came into being.

Bonus Tracks
'When She Comes' (Hammill)
'Masks' (Hammill)

These two tracks are live-in-studio renditions recorded for the John Peel Show on BBC Radio 1 on 11 November 1976. Note the connection of the date to the title of the first track on *The Least We Can Do Is Wave to Each Other*. Coincidence? Both performances are faithful to the originals, and, unlike the bonus tracks on the reissues of *Godbluff* and *Still Life*, don't suffer from poor recording quality.

The Quiet Zone / The Pleasure Dome (1977)

Personnel:
Guy Evans: drums and percussion
Peter Hammill: vocals, piano, guitar
David Jackson: saxophone
Nic Potter: bass
Graham Smith: violin, viola
Charles Dickie (on bonus tracks): cello, keyboards
Produced at Rockfield Studios, May – June 1977 by Peter Hammill
UK release date and label: September 1977; Charisma. US release date and label:
1992; Caroline.
Running time: 43:34

In 1977, with David Jackson and Hugh Banton leaving the fold, it became
clear that Van der Graaf couldn't keep going as it had – something had to
change. For Hammill and Evans, quitting wasn't an option. They both felt
that there was more to be discovered using the uniquely idiosyncratic VdGG
method.

Hammill approached violinist and former member of String Driven Thing,
Graham Smith. The violin was a very Van der Graafian instrument, to be
sure, but Smith's approach to the instrument was sufficiently unconventional
to qualify him as a true heir to the VdGG frontline. Smith would provide
a strong lead instrument where Jackson's saxes had dominated the
proceedings. But there were still holes that needed plugging: with Banton
gone, there was a need for a bass presence as well as something to offset the
gaping hole that the departure of the organ would create. As far as the bass
went, Hammill was able to convince Nic Potter to return to the fold.

For his own part, Hammill decided to step up his role in the band, taking
the role of lead guitarist, along with the non-organ keyboard work and vocals
he had been accustomed to. The band as it now was, an ungainly four-piece,
had a surprising amount of power as evinced by their live performances,
attributable in no small part to Potter's newfound extreme bass sound, jaw-
dropping in its ferocious intensity. The new line-up of the band, working
under the abbreviated name of Van der Graaf, had songs that were similarly
short in length, in comparison to the earlier catalogue. They were now FM
radio-friendly, with a directness and punch that eluded the earlier material,
without sacrificing any of the complexity that VdG had become known for.

Charisma had provided cover art, and so had the band – each party
unaware of the other's intent to contribute. The band and the label each
liked both efforts, and so it was decided that they should adorn the front
and back covers of the album, making each side seem like the cover. To that
end, the album was represented somewhat like two extended-play records,
each side being represented by a different title: 'The Quiet Zone' and 'The
Pleasure Dome'.

'Lizard Play' (Hammill)

The opening track counts in the new VdG sound – a somewhat fragile, skittish high-end anchored by an outsized, imposing rhythm section, and lyrics that are markedly more personal, if not necessarily autobiographical, than those on earlier albums. Like many of the songs on this release, 'Lizard Play' examines the complexities of interpersonal relationships, and the benefits of being open compared to those of being guarded at the outset of a romantic affair. Hammill's acoustic guitar intro is unlike anything he'd produced up to that point; the addition of the bass, drums, and violin a few seconds later steer the song into art-funk territory – the bass is aggressive but at the same time, slinky, and Evans, with an unusually varied amount of embellishing additions to his drum kit, adds to the rhythm's clever sinew.

'The Habit of the Broken Heart' (Hammill)

As in 'Lizard Play', Hammill counts in the tune with an acoustic guitar riff-call that Smith's violin responds to. When the rest of the band joins, the result is a far less funky affair than the first song, however. The first part of the song plods slowly, almost dirge-like. Potter's bass thumps morosely, and Evans's drumming is more energetic and sprightlier, but not enough to pull the song out of the gloom it's mired in. Just before the four-minute mark, however, the trajectory changes along with a shift in Hammill's lyrical approach. Cajoling rather than descriptive, the words are buttressed by a more engaged violin/bass attack, finally accepting Evans's invitation to soar. The soaring is all too brief, though, and the funereal pace beckons again and takes the song into its closing moments. Though this song has seen a much longer half-life in performance than 'Lizard Play', it's not nearly as inspired.

'The Siren Song' (Hammill)

Another song that's been a consistent part of solo Hammill concerts (often the opener), 'The Siren Song' begins more like a solo effort, with Hammill singing and accompanying himself on piano right out of the gate. A common lyrical motif throughout the album is probably most acutely examined here – the nature of attraction/addiction to and obsession with various intangible concerns – sex, adventure, youth and immortality, religion, etc.

The song is imbued with high drama. There are some wild passages featuring complex violin and bass interplay where Potter maintains a level of ferocity and agility simultaneously. It's an intense piece that tends toward the white-knuckled inward stock-taking that is a central part of so much of Hammill's work, and the Homeric allusions of nautical peril, with pitch-perfect accompaniment from the band, makes the sea spit on the cold guard-handles of the deck seem almost real.

'Last Frame' (Hammill)

Another powerful, dramatic song, and a far cry from the artfully clever and tentative dance of 'Lizard Play'. 'Last Frame' is a very confident, almost strident, showcase of the band's strengths, starting with an extended instrumental stretch featuring Nic Potter and Graham Smith on bass and violin. Hammill eventually arrives on the scene in a spoken introduction that quickly morphs into singing, and playing electric guitar, which sounds quite different from the *World Record* axe workouts, and closer to the some of the solos on *Over*, but no less dark and eerie than the latter. Strummed acoustic guitar embellishments rise and fall away throughout the course of the song. The eeriness is compounded by the instrumental outro, which again features Potter and Smith, but with Evans providing a consistently irregular pulse, sounding like they're already at the juncture where progressive rock meets post-punk, even though it's only 1977. Dark stuff that smacks of a soundtrack looking for a worthy film. And, in fact, photography is the working metaphor in this song: the protagonist self-identifies as an amateur photographer, and the assertions and suppositions made about the person he's addressing come to light via the process of film development.

'The Wave' (Hammill)

'The Wave' aside, the songs on the 'Pleasure Dome' side of the album (Side B) are generally more upbeat than those on the 'Quiet Zone' side (musically at least), but 'The Wave' is a beautifully understated short piece of music with some of the most incisive lyrics Hammill has committed to paper.

Tackling in earnest for the first time a subject he would return to quite often, Hammill writes and sings of the complexities and difficulties inherent in the act of human communication, as well as the paradox of language. The metaphors utilised, though – sea, sand, waves – are well-traversed lyrical territory. In similar fashion to 'The Siren Song', Hammill opens 'The Wave' with vocals and piano, almost immediately accompanied by mournful strains from Smith's violin, and by Evans and Potter shortly after. It quickly becomes very atmospheric, with treated violin and tightly controlled bass feedback strains that almost sound like a cor anglais.

'Cat's Eye / Yellow Fever (Running)' (Hammill, Smith)

'Cat's Eye' began life as an instrumental composition by Graham Smith, written while he was between jobs – his earlier band, String-Driven Thing (also on the Charisma label), had broken up, but he'd not yet joined Van der Graaf. Hammill heard it and wrote lyrics, and the rest was history. Unsurprisingly, given its history, it opens with propulsive violin work from Smith, both bowed and pizzicato, with Evans, Potter and Hammill, on guitar, jumping into the already moving car.

As the band continues at a furious pace, Hammill lays down a text that seems to be a reminiscence of angry defiance of norms and expectations from a not-too-distant past self – perhaps looking back at Rikki Nadir? The pace does not last for long, and everything seems to implode, replaced by a mournful dirge led by multi-tracked violin, that carries on for several minutes, slowly decaying and disintegrating into bizarrely placid feedback. This song was released as a 7" single, in France, with the abbreviated title of 'Cat's Eye'.

'The Sphinx in the Face' (Hammill)

This is another song whose lyrics, at first, take a look at the desires and aspirations of a disaffected, rebellious youth. Soon, however, the narrative skips to the present-tense, focussing on the seemingly irreconcilable differences between the longing for future adventure and experience and the desire to *have had* adventures and experiences. Musically, the tune mirrors the lyrics change for change. It begins with an uncharacteristically funky lead guitar attack punctuated by Potter's bass note bombs, but before long, morphs into an intense display of piano-driven rock (Hammill's guitar comes back in, but it's no longer at the forefront of the sonic field). This is followed by a brief passage of lament where the intensity drops off, and Hammill's narrator seems to verge dangerously close to self-pity. The band bounces back, however, fully refuelled and with an instrumentally fleshed-out reprise of the song's opening theme. Over this bit of wild and fierce playing, Hammill repeats, with all the inscrutability of the Sphinx, the final, paradoxical refrain: 'Such a drag to be told / You're so here, you're so gone, you're so young / So old, so near, so wrong…'. David Jackson makes a brief appearance towards the end of the song (the album's credits list him as providing 'sphinx-like inserts'. The band fades out, leaving Hammill alone, stage centre, as he continues to repeat that mantra-like refrain.

'Chemical World' (Hammill)

'Chemical World' is the last fully-formed song on the album and gets to the heart of the 'pleasure dome' experience. It opens with Hammill singing the part of a cajoling, wheedling enabler, and the acoustic guitar and violin intro puts forth a sense of pastoral whimsy. As the same narrative voice returns to say later in the song, though, 'It doesn't last…' and the band kicks in with appropriate menace. The tune becomes a visceral depiction of the effects of the pleasure centre of the brain being artificially stimulated; the drugs distort and derange any sense of time. Long, slow passages marked by acoustic guitar strums and thundering bass riffs accentuate the feeling of helpless ennui that is described in the lyrics.

Surrounded by all this is the hallucinatory middle section, with multi-tracked and distorted vocals from Hammill making the words almost as unintelligible as the soliloquy in the earlier 'Magog'. Guy Evans really shines in this section, with his own multi-tracked drumming sounding like a lead instrument, and in fact, Evans propels the tune out of the addled chaos into a storming rave-up over which Hammill declaims the perils of trying to exist in such a 'world'. It's a hellishly effective album closer.

'The Sphinx Returns' (Hammill)

Of course, technically, 'Chemical World' doesn't close the album. That honour belongs to the brief snippet 'The Sphinx Returns'. As the title implies, it's a reprise of 'The Sphinx in the Face'. Where the playing at the end of the original song fades out, leaving Hammill to sing unaccompanied, the reverse occurs here: both singer and band come in playing the 'Sphinx' outro riff, but this time the vocals fade away, and the band continue to play, with a sense of glee just this side of rapturous abandon that makes it abundantly clear that this iteration of Van der Graaf can still generate electric positivity. David Jackson again joins in, and the mixing of violin and saxophone is a wonder to behold.

Bonus Tracks
'Door' (Hammill)
'Ship of Fools' (Hammill)
'The Wave (Demo)' (Hammill)

Both 'Door' and 'Ship of Fools' were recorded around the time of the recording sessions for *The Quiet Zone / The Pleasure Dome*, but were left off the album. They feature the band's newest member, Charles Dickie, who added his parts to the already completed tracks, on cello and keyboards. 'Door' featured a heavy dose of Dickie's keyboard work, and it, like 'Ship of Fools', sported a more 'metal' sound.

'Ship of Fools' was placed on the B-side of the *Cat's Eye* single, and made its digital debut on the 1993 Virgin Records compilation, *I Prophesy Disaster*, before finally ending up on this CD reissue. 'Door', on the other hand, didn't get an official release, in any format, until the VdGG retrospective box set released by Virgin in 2000. They were, of course, both featured on the 1978 live Van der Graaf album, *Vital*.

Both songs had relatively straightforward lyrics from Hammill. 'Ship of Fools' was a metaphor-laden description of the denizens of the eponymous ship, evidently sailing towards a dystopian hellscape, and 'Door' was a sort of micro-fiction about a 'he' and 'she' in a room which only one of them wants to leave.

The demo version of 'The Wave' presented here is an instrumental track that doesn't appear to vary at all from the final version. It's worth noting that the song, in embryonic form, was first introduced by Hammill at a solo concert in 1976.

Vital (1978)

Personnel:
Charles Dickie: cello, electric piano, synthesizer
Guy Evans: drums
Peter Hammill: vocals, piano, guitar
David Jackson: saxophones and flute
Nic Potter: bass
Graham Smith: violin
Produced at Foel Studio, Spring, 1978, by Guy Evans.
UK release date and label: July 1978; Charisma. US release date and label: 1978; PVC.
Running time: 1:26:14

The decision to release a double live album was not reached lightly, particularly for Hammill, who was, at the time, not a fan of concert recordings. He felt that the experience of a live gig belonged to those in attendance – the audience and the performers – and that the essence of the event could never truly be committed to record. But Van der Graaf were on the ropes financially, and the release of a live album was seen as something that could help the band survive. In this sense, the album title was entirely appropriate! Another concern that Hammill had was doing right by the record-buying public; he didn't like the idea of fans shelling out money to buy an album that contained songs that were already present on other albums that they likely owned. Thus, it was decided that a sizable portion of the new album should contain songs that hadn't yet seen a proper studio album release.

Vital was recorded during the second night of Van der Graaf's two-night stint at the Marquee in London, on 16 January 1978. David Jackson was invited to join the five-piece as a special guest, but due to technical recording difficulties, he almost didn't make it onto the album. Guy Evans was in charge of recording the shows and then mixing the album, with help from Dave Anderson, a friend of the band who ran Foel Studio. The two inexperienced sound engineers mastered the learning curve and eventually got the recordings ready for commercial release.

The album was released in July of that year by Charisma in the United Kingdom and parts of Europe; Philips picked up the European slack. In the United States, Mercury had dropped the band, and a record company named PVC picked up the album for stateside release. The Charisma and Philips jackets were in a gatefold format, showcasing a photo collage of band members and associates on the inside cover, while the PVC editions came as a single pouch that held both records. The initial CD release in 1989 had its own complications: while the Japanese release contained the entire recording on two discs, the European version of the rerelease was limited to one disc with a maximum duration of 80 minutes, necessitating the deletion of certain tracks. Most of these contained the entire album minus two tracks, but some went as far as cutting fully half of the album. To confuse the issue further, the printed tracklist that accompanied these latter CDs indicated that all ten of the album's original tracks were present. The situation was resolved, finally, with the 2005 Virgin reissue.

Cellist/keyboardist Charles Dickie was brought on board the Van der Graaf ship just after *Quiet Zone* was completed, to enhance and widen the string palette, and to add a second layer of keyboards to complement Hammill's piano. The recently retooled band had already been astounding audiences with their furious performances, and the five-piece version lent more dynamics to the sonic attack without lessening the effect. It made sense to document the live VdG experience.

After eight studio albums, it was certainly time for the world beyond the touring circuit to experience the 'live' side of Van der Graaf, and the album was met with wide acclaim, selling more copies than any VdG or VdGG album to date! The sound is raw, matching the primal energy of the performance; it's safe to say that most fans of prog rock had never heard anything quite this extreme.

'Ship of Fools' (Hammill)

The band seemingly hit the stage running; there's no building up of intensity – it's all there at the outset. It's almost beyond belief, in fact, that Hammill's voice isn't completely shot after these first six minutes. In actuality, 'Ship of Fools' was the third song of the evening's performance. The band opened with the one-two punch of 'Cat's Eye' and 'The Sphinx in the Face' from the recent album *The Quiet Zone / The Pleasure Dome*.

This live rendition is three minutes longer than the studio version. Graham Smith's violin replaces the high-pitched guitar overdubs, leaving Hammill to concentrate on the lead. His vocals on the studio version are markedly subdued by the muscular sound of the band, but here, he dominates the scene, while the rest of Van der Graaf still sounds exponentially more menacing than they did on the 'Cat's Eye' B-side. Otherwise, the performance is faithful to the original, as far as the original length of the song goes. After that three-and-a-half-minute mark which would normally be the song's fade-out point, VdG launches into an instrumental run that is gradually reduced to Dickie's and Smith's strings and harmonics from Hammill's guitar, before the entire ensemble kick in for a reprise of the opening riff and a final rave-up that is evidently very much a crowd-pleaser.

'Still Life' (Hammill)

Van der Graaf's live rendition of 'Still Life' equals and perhaps at times surpasses the original in magnificent gloom. As with everything else on *Vital*, the playing verges on the extreme. The version found on the eponymous 1976 album wasn't sterile, by any means, but Banton's organ keyboard accompaniment of Hammill's vocals are very bright and clean in comparison to the somewhat murky pairing of violin and cello that provide the backdrop to the long introductory (fully one-third of the track's ten minutes) soliloquy. When the full band finally does enter the fray, the resulting explosion of pent-up energy is as glorious as the classic four-piece VdGG's version.

'Last Frame' (Hammill)

The third song of the evening from *The Quiet Zone* / *The Pleasure Dome*, but the first one on the album, 'Last Frame', like 'Ship of Fools', is also substantially extended to three minutes beyond the length of the original version. Graham Smith begins the proceedings with a violin solo that's only hinted at in the introduction to the studio version, underpinned by Nic Potter's weaponised bass. In similar fashion, the lead-in to the final section, which showcases Potter's playing, is extended, giving the band more time to build up to a satisfying conclusion.

'Mirror Images' (Hammill)

The album's second side opens with another song that was entirely new to the VdG(G) catalogue. 'Mirror Images' would eventually find a home on Peter Hammill's 1979 solo album, *pH7*. The solo version is very keyboard/synth-wash heavy, and much more compact and streamlined than its younger counterpart. If the 'Vital' version of 'Mirror Images' feels unfinished in comparison to the later *pH7* recording, it's also more complex and adventurous, and, ultimately, more enjoyable.

Charles Dickie, on keyboards, begins the song, after a spoken 'M'sieur, s'il vous plait', from Hammill. The band, which now includes David Jackson on flute, begins playing. For the moment, Hammill holds off on his lead guitar attack. The music is moody and comparatively slow at first; it picks up steam eventually, but never loses the sour tone. With the second verse, Hammill brings the guitar into play, Jackson switches the flute out for his saxophone, and the whole thing sounds like it would fit nicely on the A-side of *Quiet Zone*. The most noticeable departure from the *pH7* version of the song comes near the end, when the band are charging towards the finish line (a common theme among these latter-day VdG performances), and Hammill repeats the refrain, 'Take the mirror away!' In the later version, that would be replaced with the much more unassuming 'In these mirror images of myself / there are no secrets'.

'Medley (Parts of "A Plague of Lighthouse Keepers" and "The Sleepwalkers")' (Hammill)

The next thirty minutes – two tracks stretching across the better part of two sides of vinyl – are devoted to what could be considered the centrepiece of the concert: a presentation of 'classic' VdGG songs. The first is a medley joining the first and second major iterations of the band. Two parts of 'Plague' are performed, marking the first time the piece has ever been played before an audience (barring a legendary performance recorded for television broadcast in piecemeal and edited together to give the impression of an uninterrupted event), and they're followed by the second half of 'The Sleepwalkers', the closing song on *Godbluff*.

'Plague' is represented here by the suite's opener, 'Eyewitness', and the climax preceding the denouement, 'The Clot Thickens'. The band wisely skirt the instrumental 'Pictures / Lighthouse' instrumental interlude which is bookended by 'Eyewitness' and its reprise and only go a little way into 'The Clot Thickens' before changing course for 'Sleepwalkers' territory.

The medley begins with Hammill playing a long, improvised run on piano, accompanied by Dickie and Smith on cello and violin, and Jackson on saxophone. After slightly more than a minute, the introductory riff to 'Eyewitness' is found on the piano, and the band coalesces around it. Much of the spacey psychedelic soundscape that adorned the original *Pawn Hearts* version is gone, but on stage, Van der Graaf manages to imbue the piece with its own brand of mystical gravitas. Though the introductory theme gives way to extended investigation, as does the theme connecting the two parts of 'Plague', the band ploughs through 'Eyewitness' with reckless abandon.

Of course, 'The Clot Thickens' calls for just such recklessness, and Van der Graaf is up to the task. The bowed attack of the two string players drive the galloping melody along with more precision than Hugh Banton's organ playing could have done; the interplay between Dickie and Smith and the rest of the band, particularly Jackson's also very incisive saxophone playing, bring out the intricacy of the piece. Just before the clot thickens to excess, the landscape switches from shoreline to (God)bluff.

The first part of 'Sleepwalkers' on *Godbluff* is one of the more complex VdGG pieces committed to record, and the current band wisely focuses on the second half, which plays to their strengths. Hammill remains on piano, largely reprising the keyboard part he played on the original, while the violin and the cello cover Banton's organ parts. With Potter taking care of the low-end duties that were once seen to by Banton's bass pedal work, Evans and Jackson are free to play, and play with, the parts of 'Sleepwalkers' that are rightfully theirs. As VdG finally puts 'Sleepwalkers' to bed, Hammill returns to the main piano melody of 'Eyewitness', bringing the medley full circle.

'Pioneers Over c' (Hammill, Jackson)

Van der Graaf reach back eight years and pull this epic 1970 prog rock space opera into the present, adding more than four minutes to it in the process. With Hammill's tortured guitar at the forefront, the band gives new urgency to the pathos that infuses the song. There are no keyboards here, but the effects-laden strings (particularly the cello) generate a truly spacey quality, as does the delay on Hammill's vocals, producing an echo that hits the ears a split-second before the actual sound.

VdG remain faithful to the original, despite the difference in instrumentation, although some of the instrumental sections are slightly longer. Thankfully, David Jackson is present to reprise his inimitable saxophone solo. Although there's no backwards-recording this time, the sense of claustrophobia from the 1970 version remains. It's not limited to his solo, though; it informs the entire performance.

'Sci-Finance' (Hammill)

Van der Graaf enters the final stretch of the concert with another new-to-the-world Hammill tune. 'Sci-Finance' is an aggressive calling-out of the moneyed elite who play the system to ensure that their wealth remains secure and that society's have-nots will likewise continue to be locked in poverty. In a dystopian twist that gives a nod to the pun in the title and aligns thematically with the futuristic motif of the previous song, the money-mad anti-heroes of Hammill's lyrics are stripped of their power by the techno-Mammon that they serve. The awareness of contemporary social ills in Hammill's lyrics, and their polemical quality, have their roots in the *Nadir's Big Chance* proto-punk ethos, and the dark, futuristic sensibility make them of a piece with many of the songs on his upcoming solo album, *pH7*. In fact, this song would be semi-forgotten for a decade: except for a small number of copies of *Vital* pressed in Japan in 1989, 'Sci-Finance' would be omitted from CD reissues of the album until 2005. In Fall 1988, a much different version of the song, re-titled 'Sci-Finance (Revisited)' would appear on Hammill's solo album *In a Foreign Town*, and a more energetic version closer in spirit to the earlier VdG version would appear on the 1993 live Hammill recording, *There Goes the Daylight*.

'Sci-Finance' is the most unqualified 'rock' performance on *Vital*. After a brief, gentle introduction led by the strings of Dickie and Smith, where Hammill sets the scene in semi-falsetto, the gloves abruptly come off. The guitar chords are simple and wildly combative, matched blow for blow with Nic Potter's bass, which is thrown further still into overdrive. The middle section of the song, with its jolting stops and starts, sounds like it was made to echo off the curved walls of an arena or stadium, as Hammill, with reduced to industrial-grade sandpaper, howls 'Only the money!' with righteous accusatory fury.

'Door' (Hammill)

From social commentary, Van der Graaf moves into psychodrama. 'Door' is the second of the two bonus tracks on the 2005 reissue of *The Quiet Zone / The Pleasure Dome* to appear on *Vital*. It taps directly into the energy supply provided by the previous track, and never lets up. Graham Smith's violin is a siren blaring frantically over the guitar/bass/drum attack that continually increases in tempo following the brief sung portion at the beginning. Charles Dickie, on keyboards, produces a synth sound that sounds so primitively futuristic, like a 1950s imagining of 21st Century technology, that it borders on comical. The song is a very successful show closer (Hammill's early 1980s K Group would often end concerts with it). Of course, there is an encore...

'Urban / Killer / Urban' (Banton, Hammill, Smith)

Having dispensed with the medley format, Van der Graaf now tries its hand at interpolation. 'Urban' was one of the songs written in the period just prior to *Godbluff*, but apparently never recorded. The 1975-76 four-piece iteration of the band played it often in encores, however. The lyrics are of a piece with Hammill's reflections on the pros and cons of city life on *The Quiet Zone / The Pleasure Dome*, but they come down pretty strongly on the 'anti' side.

The band begins the song with a coy playfulness as Hammill teases the melody on guitar. Nic Potter's bass rolls and cascades through the performance like ocean waves. At the five-minute mark, Jackson, Dickie and Smith stay their hands, and Hammill arpeggiates over Potter's and Evans's rhythm, until, of a sudden, all six players explode into 'Killer'. (To be clear, they're playing the middle section of 'Killer', which itself was taken from the Heebalob song 'A Cloud As Big As a Man's Hand', recorded as a demo for the Chris Judge Smith band a year prior to its release on *H to He Who Am the Only One*.) The combination of sax and strings in this section is one of the high points of the concert. With one run-through of the vocal-less 'Killer' section and the refrain that follows it behind them, the band cuts back to 'Urban' for the final ninety seconds.

'Nadir's Big Chance' (Hammill)

Van der Graaf end the concert, the album, and, in effect, their 1970s recorded legacy, with this glorious slab of noise. The title track of Hammill's 1975 solo album is rendered in a wildly celebratory and anarchic fashion, with Hammill fully committing to the reprisal of his alter-ego, Rikki Nadir. While Charles Dickie's cello takes the role of second guitar, Smith and Jackson soar over the top. Jackson's bleats and honks during the middle instrumental section sound like he's trying to intone the eponymous phrase though the saxophone. Serious fun, indeed!

'The refugees are gone; they take their separate paths...'

So, where'd everybody go? Hugh Banton was already gone from Van der Graaf by the end of 1976 when VdGG was about to become VdG, and still counted Peter Hammill and Guy Evans among its members, with David Jackson in auxiliary status. Of the four core VdGG members, Banton became the most removed from the music business as he knew it from the standpoint of a recording and touring musician. He remained closely involved in music in other ways, turning his attention full-time to building and developing organs, primarily for church installation. His company, The Organ Workshop, was founded in 1992, and as of 2020 is still active.

Banton's post-1976 forays back into the world of professional music-making were few. He wasn't heard from again until 1985 when he resurfaced to record an album with Jackson and Evans, *Gentlemen Prefer Blues*. This album has been long out of print and was never released on CD, although six of its eight songs were cannibalised for the unauthorised release of an album, *Now and Then*, on LP and CD, incorrectly attributed to Van der Graaf Generator. He's released three solo albums: two interpretations of Bach, and a performance of Gustav Holst's *The Planets*. The two Bach recordings were *The Goldberg Variations,* in 2002, on CD, and *HB Plays JSB on HB3* in 2019, digital-only (HB3 is the name of the most current model of Banton's self-designed organ, which has been with him in some form since the early 1970s!). The Holst album was released on CD in 2009.

While Evans and Jackson kept close ties with Hammill, Banton only appeared on two of his post-1976 solo albums: 1986's *Skin*, and *Everyone You Hold*, from 1997. On the former, he played a cello-esque keyboard part for the song 'All Said and Done', and on the latter, he returned to the classic VdGG organ sound for a duet with Hammill's electric piano on 'Bubble'. In 1997, Banton appeared on the CD, *The Union Chapel Concert*, which was the recorded document of a gig put on by Evans and Hammill, after Evans was invited by the Union Chapel to organise and curate a show. In addition to playing on renditions of two Hammill songs, 'Red Shift' and 'Traintime', and performing 'Lemmings' with the classic VdGG line-up, he did a solo organ performance of Samuel Barber's 'Adagio for Strings'.

Although not a full-fledged member any longer, Jackson still made contributions to the final two Van der Graaf albums, *The Quiet Zone* / *The Pleasure Dome*, and *Vital*. Jackson stayed connected to Hammill, playing on almost all of his solo albums from 1978's *The Future Now* through to *Incoherence* in 2004. Solo Hammill albums after the VdGG reunion have not contained any contributions from Jackson. He did make his own contribution to *The Union Chapel Concert*: an 11-minute medley of solo material.

Jackson kept busy, musically, in other ways following the VdGG dissolution, touring with Peter Gabriel's band in 1978 and 1979, and occasionally with

Hammill in the early 1980s and mid-1990s, working with Guy Evans and Nic Potter on the 'Long Hello' series of albums (*The Long Hello 3*, the only one to not have a CD reissue, was Jackson's project). More importantly, he focused on solo work, writing and recording music for theatre, and his own Soundbeam invention, which responded to motion and was used therapeutically to assist disabled children. Highlights of his recorded output include his *Tonewall Stands* and *Fractal Bridge* albums from 1992 and 1993, respectively, and his 2018 collaboration with ex-King Crimson violinist David Cross, *Another Day*. Currently, he is a member of the prog rock group Kaprekar's Constant.

Guy Evans rivalled Jackson for most wide-ranging post-VdGG musical projects, joining Mother Gong and Amon Düül II in the early 1980s, and co-founding the experimental music collective Echo City around the same time. He worked with Nic Potter on the second 'Long Hello' album, and oversaw the fourth and final one, along with David Jackson and another group he was involved with, Life of Riley. These were released in 1981 and 1983, respectively.

Evans guested on a number of post-1978 Hammill albums, but not nearly as consistently as Jackson. Nevertheless, he was an integral part of Hammill's K Group, the recording and touring band that existed from 1981-1985. In 1988, Evans and Hammill co-released the album *Spur of the Moment*, an experimental and improvisational recording. Predating the VdGG reunion by a few years, he's been a member of the art-rock group The Subterraneans since 2002.

Peter Hammill, of course, has accomplished enough in music in the interim between the split and reformation of Van der Graaf Generator to fill another book! Suffice to say that he's released over thirty albums during that period, toured extensively, completed an opera version of Edgar Allan Poe's *The Fall of the House of Usher*, and found time to act in the role of guest musician on numerous occasions, working with the likes of Robert Fripp, Peter Gabriel, Moondog, Ayuo Takahashi, The Stranglers, David Cross, and the Italian prog band, Premiata Forneria Marconi.

Present (2005)

Personnel:
Hugh Banton: organ, bass guitar
Guy Evans: drums
Peter Hammill: vocals, electric guitar, electric piano
David Jackson: saxophone, flute, Soundbeam
Produced at Pyworthy Rectory, Terra Incognita, and The Organ Workshop,
February 2004, by Van der Graaf Generator.
UK release date and label: April 2005; Virgin.
Highest chart places: UK 103 Germany: 100
Running time: 1:02:05

In April 2005, the reformed Van der Graaf Generator, consisting of the four
core members – Banton, Evans, Hammill, and Jackson – released their first
album in almost three decades. *Present* had its beginnings in an exploratory
weeklong session during February 2004, during which the band came up with
the six songs that comprise the first disc of the 2 CD set. The four musicians
had made plans to do something together in 2003, but in December of
that year, Hammill suffered a heart attack, and all bets were off. Happily, he
recovered quickly and completely, and that event only served to strengthen
the band's conviction that reforming, sooner rather than later, was the right
way forward. While most of the songs on the first disc are credited to Hammill,
putting the material together was much more of a real-time group effort than
it ever had been for the band. In the past, Hammill had brought most of the
songs almost fully-formed, and it was up to the rest of the band to complete
them. With the songs on *Present*, Hammill worked with the other three
members from the outset on the writing process.

Virgin Records, which had long since absorbed the now-defunct Charisma
label catalogue, was eager to make the VdGG reunion, leading to a record
that they could release, a reality. Their eagerness was justified: *Present* sold
amazingly well, with Virgin providing some serious advertising muscle. Adding
a second disc consisting entirely of instrumental improvisations might not
seem like a terribly wise move for a band just returning to the public eye after
so many years, but this *was* Van der Graaf – a band which, while never really
flouting convention, didn't exactly embrace it either. Perhaps they were at last
getting satisfaction for the aborted *Pawn Hearts* double LP!

'Every Bloody Emperor' (Hammill)
Present starts off with Hammill's scathing indictment of political world leaders
at the start of the 21st Century. No names are used, but it's hard not to see
American president George W. Bush or British Prime Minister David Cameron
in one's mind's eye while listening to the eloquent indictments contained
in the lyrics. Like Hammill's attention to contemporary concerns, while
employing the method of rhetorically complex lyrical explorations that he used

to such great effect on *Godbluff* and *Still Life*, the band coalesce magnificently as the VdGG of old, but manage to sound utterly modern. Banton's organ set-up sounds light years more advanced than what fans last heard on *World Record* in 1976, Hammill's complimentary keyboard sounds much more like what's been heard on recent solo albums, and Jackson's sax still contains the old element of danger, but the old chaotic energy sounds a lot more finely-honed. This is the sound of a band that has forgotten nothing, but is not bound to the past. The prominent use of the word 'emperor' throws a spotlight on the old 1970 VdGG chestnut 'The Emperor in His War-Room'. As has been noted elsewhere in this book, neither Guy Evans nor Peter Hammill were particularly keen on the song. Contrasting the 2005 'Emperor' with its predecessor, one can see just how much the band, and Hammill in particular as a lyricist, has grown.

'Boleas Panic' (Jackson)

David Jackson wrote this instrumental on his own, and, as such, it stands alone among the songs on this album. It was composed following the band's decision to reunite, in the run-up to the rehearsals of material for the new album. Jackson was inspired by a film about gauchos, or South American cowboys, who used a weapon known as a bolas – weights attached to a rope – for hunting and herding. Unfortunately, or fortunately, Jackson misremembered the term, and called his piece 'Bolero Boleas', as it was based on a 3/4 bolero rhythm.

When it came time to record their material for 'Present', the band ran through two takes of Jackson's composition. According to the composer, 'The first version was calmer and more structured and had a more Celtic feel. On another day, we found ourselves playing it again in a much more aggressive and haphazard way. Fortunately, we were in record. For the album, we chose this second version and PH gave it the name of 'Boleas Panic''.

Jackson begins the song with some plaintive sax, but things quickly turn sinister with the introduction of Hammill's electric guitar distortion and feedback. His guitar sound and playing is as off-kilter and wonderfully abrasive as it was during the band's 1975-76 period, but it, too, has become more nuanced. While all four band members play with purpose and spirit, it is Jackson's vehicle. His sax provides the melody and he solos over the driving, juddering rhythm that occasionally veers ever so slightly into reggae territory. Despite it being a composed piece, 'Boleas Panic' is about as close as the entire band ever got to a song-based improvisation.

'Nutter Alert' (Hammill)

This song, along with 'Every Bloody Emperor' are the surviving gems of *Present* that have enjoyed a post-album release life in VdGG setlists. 'Nutter' is as raucous and unabashed as 'Every Bloody Emperor' is stately and majestic, and it owes much to the 'Rikki Nadir' persona. A distant yell can be heard cuing the song in, and the band bursts out of the gate – Jackson parping and honking over the twin keyboard attack from Banton and Hammill, and Evans pushing the cart with his thundering drum attack.

The recording of Hammill's vocals sounds decidedly compressed and lo-fi. This is not a bad thing; it adds to the immediacy and spirit of the song, a playfully vitriolic second-person diatribe against someone who apparently has a penchant for the ego-driven derailing of otherwise pleasant situations: 'And how contorted is that logic you so forcefully exert / You're a car-crash in the making'. Relentless, good, cathartic fun, it plays like the less-inhibited cousin to Hammill's song from a few years prior, 'Tango for One'.

'Abandon Ship!' (Evans, Hammill)
'Abandon Ship!' is another cantankerous, noisy slice of fun. Less hard-driving than bombastically lurching, this is the first of many 21st Century VdGG songs that have a lyrical preoccupation with mortality and ageing. Hammill counts the tune in on heavily effect-laden guitar, while the other three musicians dance around the perimeter. Eventually, Jackson and Banton bear down on the lead, while Hammill swings in and out of the quirky melody. Clearly, the band is having a great time, bouncing riffs and runs off one another.

Lyrically, the song is also approached with a sense of humour. Although only in their 50s at this point, the band apparently felt that to not somehow face the question of longevity would be disingenuous, but it's faced with a gleam in the collective eye. Hammill sings of the occupants of a ship of fools that's different than the one in the 1970s Van der Graaf song, or perhaps it's the same one twenty-five years later. 'It's difficult to think of anything less magic than the aged in pursuit of the hip;' even here Hammill is punning, perhaps, on the double meaning of 'hip' as it applies to someone of elderly status. The sailors have been on this ship for so long that they've forgotten their identities – a classic Hammill trope – and so find themselves on the 'Sloop John Doe'! The change from the third to first person in the lyrics is disconcerting, but implies a sense of self-awareness at last, of their condition, if not their identity: 'And it's difficult to think of anything that's factual / now we find ourselves in Alzheimer's grip… we're all anonymous on this one'.

'In Babelsberg' (Hammill)
Back in serious territory, 'In Babelsberg' is a contemporary slice-of-life account of the titular film studio district situated near Berlin. Musically, it's very hard-driving; Hammill and Jackson, on guitar and sax respectively, play the introduction in near-perfect unison before departing into separate and more complex parts. Banton's presence here is mainly on the low end, as he and Evans provide the rhythmic pulse. Between the quasi-verses, there's some exceptional soloing from Hammill as he trades barbs with Jackson. It sounds

very 'live'. Lyrically, beyond the descriptions of goings-on in Germany, this is a philosophical meditation on how our sense of history impacts our perceptions. Looking for the Babelsberg he once knew, Hammill's narrator's reaction runs from bemusement to confusion. It's worth noting that in 2004, Hammill released a dense and complex single-track solo album titled *Incoherence*, and the first part of the epic work, which deals with the failings of language, references the Tower of Babel.

'On the Beach' (Hammill, Jackson)

This last track on the 'song' disc of *Present* is quite a departure for the band. It's a mellow slice of jazz-rock, primarily keyboard-led. For the greater part of the first minute, we can hear the band jokingly discussing what they're about to play, likening it to The Beach Boys' 'Sloop John B'. Hammill can be heard comparing the piece to other Beach Boys material: '...much more towards a cross between cool jazz and 'Surfin' Safari'. Evans adds that there's a 'slightly sinister vibe... somewhat "Surf's Up".'

As the band humorously share their thoughts, Hammill and Banton, on keyboards and organ, start to define the song's melody, and Hammill begins singing as Jackson makes a gentle appearance on soprano sax. Evans comes in a bit later, also gently. The sung part of the song is relatively short, and, with a nod to 'Wondering', a line from the song's lyrics, 'Even the Silver Surfer agrees...' is brought back and sung in repetition by Hammill, multi-tracked in many registers, from a falsetto soprano down through to basso. The two keyboards and sax trade off on the main melody, and eventually fade out, replaced by a field recording of surf noise.

Yes, the Silver Surfer (a Marvel Comics character whose heyday dates from the time of the band's early days) is present in the lyrics, and Hammill seems to be engaging in dialogue with his younger self. In 'Orthenthian St', from the band's first album, he sings 'I feel a calling for the sea, I want to walk on the sand dunes; I hope you'll forgive me if I say I can't take you', while in the present song, we hear 'Right now I want to walk towards the sea, hoping you're still in step with me'. The general vibe of the song is an exhortation to acknowledge one's journey, and its costs, without being tied to it. 'Ah, come on', Hammill shouts, with a voice full of equanimity and anticipation, 'Surf's up'!

The second disc of the 'Present' album consists entirely of VdGG improvisations. While fascinating, and at the very least, entertaining, they don't really bear in-depth analysis in the same way as the songs. It's more effective to discuss them as one body of work, which I'll do here.

With a few shorter exceptions, all of these pieces are as long as the songs on the first disc. They all have a very 'live' feel, and all four band members are pushing the envelope, often simultaneously. The playing is intuitive, and for each musician, there's a degree of sympathetic listening that's balanced by a confident, intrepid desire to explore and define their space in relation to the other three. This is new ground for the band; the riffs that are improvised on haven't been heard before, with one exception: 'Slo Moves' contains David Jackson's soprano sax part from Peter Hammill's solo song, 'Oasis', which appeared on his 1992 *Fireships* album.

Trisector (2008)

Personnel:
Hugh Banton: organ, bass guitar
Guy Evans: drums, percussion
Peter Hammill: vocals, piano, electric guitar
Produced at The Gaia Centre, July 2007 by Van der Graaf Generator
UK release date and label: March 2008; Virgin.
Running time: 53:45

Three years after the release of *Present*, and after the departure of David Jackson, who'd been on every VdGG album but *The Aerosol Grey Machine*, the now-trio released *Trisector*. Overall, a more immediate and collaborative group of songs, the material on *Trisector* continued the trend begun with *Present* towards shorter songs. It's worth noting that all three band members share writing credits for eight out of nine songs on the album.

Beginning a trend toward referencing the wilder side of mathematics in the band's song titles and lyrics, *Trisector* refers to a legendary unsolvable geometry problem – trisecting an angle (constructing a new angle equal to one third of an existing angle, or dividing an angle into three equal parts) using only a compass and straightedge. It's an interesting metaphor for the work of a trio of musicians trying to figure out how to carry on with the loss of an integral fourth member.

Prior to the release of the album in 2008, Banton, Evans, and Hammill had agreed to make a go of VdGG as a trio in a live context. They toured in 2007, road-testing two new songs that would eventually end up on 'Trisector', but they were still unsure as to whether the next step of recording a new album was at all feasible. They met up in a fashion similar to the reunion of the four-piece in 2003, and once again were pleased with the prospects of moving forward.

The bulk of the album, minus post-recording overdubs, was completed in two weeks at a disued complex that at one time served as an alternative energy museum. The trio were able to use one of the larger rooms as a makeshift studio, and went to work on recording fully-formed songs and fine-tuning the nascent pieces.

'The Hurlyburly' (Banton, Evans, Hammill)
As on the previous album, *Trisector* has one instrumental. This time, though, it's the lead-off track. Picking up where the last song on *Present* left off, the band continue to explore their apparent fascination with surf rock. 'The Hurlyburly' sounds less like prog and more like a slower-tempo version of The Ventures – particularly the song 'Walk, Don't Run' – right down to the introductory drum fill.

The outré, psychedelic sound of Hammill's guitar is gone. 'The Hurlyburly' features a relatively clean guitar tone, and a similarly straightforward and

93

uncomplicated organ sound from Banton. There's a long intro wherein Hammill builds up tension by repeating a short, arpeggiated riff before releasing the band into full flow.

'Interference Patterns' (Banton, Evans, Hammill)

Here, the trio goes from a vibe of blissful surf rock to a fiendishly complex prog workout worthy of the name Van der Graaf Generator. According to Hammill, the band had initially discovered the central riff during an improv session and unintentionally altered the time signature. Hammill later discovered that playing the riff in both time signatures against each other 'produced a third, phantom, riff'. Amazingly, the band has been able to play the piece live, and pull it off, which requires each musician to focus on their own internal count and trust that they'll end up at the same time/place as the others. Not unlike much of the 1970s VdGG material, but certainly taken to extremes. The lyrics involve the story of a nineteenth-century scientist's discovery, which leads, in the song, to a meditation on what quantum physics might tell us about our existence and fate.

'The Final Reel' (Banton, Evans, Hammill)

The contemporary VdGG 'sound' began to be defined with 'The Final Reel'. Many of the songs on subsequent albums seem to find common ground here. Lyrically, it could easily slide into place on a Peter Hammill solo album. Focusing once again on the spectre of mortality, the ageing couple around whom the lyrics revolve appear to be contemplating acting on a suicide pact. Dance and cinema are both titular references here, and long-time Hammill followers might be reminded of two songs in particular from the early 1980s: 'Film Noir' and 'The Great Experiment'. The latter, in particular, also examines the death-wish.

A dark song, indeed, and the music reflects that. It opens with a minute-long series of halting, tentative piano runs from Hammill, and a very subdued accompaniment from Banton on organ, which is set to approximate a flute sound. Banton also plays bass guitar here, giving the low end a bit more of an attack than is afforded from his usual bass pedal playing. Evans provides very minimal time-keeping.

Following the introduction, the trio bears down and begins the song in earnest. The tempo picks up, thanks to Evans, and Banton switches to an organ setting more in keeping with the overall feel of the piece. Hammill presses on with the piano, but his growling guitar fills adorn some of the sparser sections. The vocals walk a line between sprightly commentary and tense apprehension. As the latter begins to overtake the former, the band responds appropriately, resulting in increasingly overpowering layers of sound in the form of added guitar tracks and the rumble of pedal-sustained piano chords. The song climaxes in a familiar VdGG workout consisting of an ebbing and flowing of all these elements.

'Lifetime' (Hammill)

This is another song that, lyrically, would fit more comfortably than most Van der Graaf songs on a solo Hammill album. It covers many of the key Hammill bases: memory, fate, relationships. 'Lifetime' is also one of two songs on *Trisector* that were finalised enough to be road-tested in live performances well before the recording sessions for the album.

The watchword for 'Lifetime' is restraint; it's an extremely quiet song, all tension until the release at the finale. The live power-trio format is accentuated here, with no noticeable overdubbing save for vocal effects; just Hammill on tastefully mordant guitar, Banton on organ and bass pedals, and Evans on cymbals and hi-hat until cutting loose at song's end. With a fairly conventional guitar solo, VdGG finds itself very far indeed from the multi-tracking studio extravaganza that was 'A Plague of Lighthouse-Keepers', but the mystery and passion at the heart of this music are still quintessentially Van der Graaf.

'Drop Dead' (Banton, Evans, Hammill)

Hammill has described this song, with respect to the rest of the album's contents, as 'a tad throwaway'. It certainly lacks the gravitas of some of the more intricate works on *Trisector*, and the lyrics, though admirable in their stance of anti-toxic masculinity, are sub-par for a writer of Hammill's calibre. And yet… it's fun! The lead organ riff is almost criminally catchy, and the interplay between it, the drums, and guitar are much more infectious than most progressive rock ever comes close to being.

Oddly, the song, in addition to being a potent earworm, is almost comically muscular. When Hammill pokes fun at the 'macho tough guy male buffoon', the music, rather than supporting the lyrical argument, becomes something of an adversary that seems to be sparring with the singer.

'Only in a Whisper' (Banton, Evans, Hammill)

This is another quiet song, with a similar live feel, though much different in style from 'Lifetime'. Banton again plays electric bass guitar, and Hammill switches to electric piano. Evans is energetic in tempo but reserved in volume. It's an exercise in simplicity, with Hammill lightly galloping and then pausing in his unswerving approach on the keyboard, conservative in his selection of notes. Banton has noted, jocularly, that in retrospect, it doesn't sound like the trio had rehearsed the tune. Like 'The Final Reel' and 'Drop Dead', it was never played live.

Lyrically, 'Only in a Whisper' is imbued with the enigmatic wordplay that marked a fair amount of earlier VdGG material. Evocative lines like 'Black dog in the desert heat will hound you', piques interest despite the bleak and hostile scene that it paints. Hammill drives the mystique home with his vocal delivery, which is at once urgent and hushed, and sung mostly at the upper end of a lower register. It really feels like the protagonist of 'Arrow' has returned to survey the 'blasted' metaphysical landscape once again.

'All That Before' (Banton, Evans, Hammill)

Along with 'Lifetime', this song was road-tested in live performances preceding the *Trisector* recording sessions, during which time it was known as 'Spex', referring to the pair of eyeglasses that are a point of concern in the lyrics. Of the two songs, 'All That Before' hews to the other end of the sonic spectrum – a loud, heavy slab of hard rock. The other thing that differentiates it from 'Lifetime' is its wink and grin. On one level, VdGG joins its alphabetical sibling Van Halen in engaging in a dialogue with The Kinks; Banton's organ lead is a prog-rock take on the 1964 classic 'You Really Got me' that will bring a smile to any British Invasion fan's face. Hammill, on fuzzed-out guitar, switches between echoing Banton's alt-Kinks lead and pursuing a second riff, with some soloing to boot.

Hammill's keenly skewed wit is also very much on display here. As Evans once wryly noted, he had to check with Hammill: 'We're really doing a song about losing one's glasses? OK!' It's an extension of the idea put forth in 'Abandon Ship!' on the band's previous album, and pursued with the same quirky irreverence: namely, the absurdities that accompany getting old. And there certainly is a sense of comic absurdism that runs through the lyrics, as the narrator fumblingly searches for his phone, his car keys, his glasses, while trying to maintain a public show of calmness and ease. As the song eventually reaches stratospheric levels of swirling Van der Graafian chaos, a la the climax of 'A Place to Survive', the mood, at last, becomes sombre – the veil is pierced, and behind all the jocular elbowing is the plaintive voice of one utterly lost in confusion.

'Over the Hill' (Banton, Evans, Hammill)

The examination of ageing, and in this instance, obsolescence, continues with the lone 'epic' track put forth by VdGG since the 2005 reunion. Clocking in at over twelve minutes, 'Over the Hill' was recorded in sections, not unlike the band's approach to 'A Plague of Lighthouse-Keepers, 37 years earlier. It originated with some demo recordings that Banton had sent to Hammill, who'd worked on them before returning them, after which Banton would do the same. The back-and-forth swapping of demos began to coalesce into what became 'Over the Hill'.

The piece soars and plummets as all the pre-21st Century extended-length VdGG compositions do, but, as a trio committed to presenting themselves as 'in the moment' as possible, multi-tracking and overdubbing are kept to a minimum, leading to a comparatively sparser final product. The organ, piano and drums leave plenty of room for each to comfortably dialogue with one another as well as the surrounding space. When it does get hairy – and of course, it does – there's still enough space between the instruments on the sonic stage for the listener to have more of a sense of clarity than would be possible in a more densely packed song like 'Childlike Faith', for instance. The band makes two such climbs toward a pinnacle of inspired chaos: the first characterised by frenetic speed, and the second by a fierce riff that sounds like it's inches away from going off the rails, and culminates in a frenzy of chord bashing that's reminiscent of the manic break in 'Man-Erg', with some particularly inspired and menacing guitar from Hammill laid the top. All this after Hammill's paroxysmal delivery of the line, 'We're still learning our lessons in the dark', which itself echoes an earlier climactic lyric from 'Childlike Faith', 'Frightened but thinking very hard / Let us make computations of the stars!' Among other things, 'Over the Hill' seems to be, lyrically, an oblique and allusive look at Van der Graaf's body of work to date.

'(We Are) Not Here' (Banton, Evans, Hammill)

Banton, Evans and Hammill wisely saved this corker of a tune for the end of the album. No time is wasted diving headlong into the central riff, which is comprised of swirling organ, thumping piano, and a wider palette in the drumkit than has been heard so far on *Trisector*. Although Banton augments the riff at various points throughout this short song, there is no departure from the insistent theme. It explodes and then trails off in the space of four minutes like an extremely vivid dream, which, according to Hammill, is how the idea for the song came to him. The lyrics, sung with an extreme gusto, are suitably dreamlike as well – highly imagistic and brief to the point of a Zen koan. There's a bit of a connection to the science-driven text of 'Interference Patterns', but ultimately 'Not Here' adheres to its own logic.

A Grounding in Numbers (2011)

Personnel:
Hugh Banton: organ, bass, harpsichord, glockenspiel, piano, guitar
Guy Evans: drums, percussion, guitar
Peter Hammill: vocals, piano, guitar, Asbury bass
Produced at The Propagation House Studios, Terra Incognita, and The Organ
Workshop, April – September 2010, by Van der Graaf Generator
UK release date and label: March 2011; Esoteric.
Running time: 48:50

Another three years passed between albums, and *A Grounding in Numbers* was released, fittingly, on 'Pi Day', 14 March 2011. Van der Graaf Generator had now been together longer than either of their stints in the 1970s! One of the keys to this longevity seemed to be that the band wasn't key to the survival of the band members and their families, nor was it omnipresent in their lives. Only when other obligations had been met did the band come together to tour or work on new material. In this way, the VdGG spirit was constantly renewed and refreshed rather than driven into the ground.

Also, in the interest of challenging each other to keep their approach to VdGG material from becoming rote, the trio decided to utilise a professional studio, rather than converting a mutually agreed upon space to suit their recording needs, as they had for *Present* and *Trisector*. That aside, the band enjoyed the same division of labour in terms of writing and arranging the material on the previous two albums. Veteran producer Hugh Padgham, known for his work on albums by The Police, and later, Sting, as well as Genesis (and Phil Collins's solo efforts), was brought in to mix the album – the first time that the band had let an outside agent into the post-production process.

But as far as performing the pieces, the band decided to step out of whatever small comfort zones they may have allowed themselves, and try their hand at other instruments. On one song, Hammill played bass, and on two other separate tracks, Banton and Evans each played guitar. VdGG also decided that, for *Grounding*, they were going to focus on shorter compositions. Never had a Van der Graaf album come close to boasting thirteen songs (even the double live album *Vital* only had ten!), nor had there been one where the longest track clocked in at just six minutes, save for *The Quiet Zone / The Pleasure Dome*, where a similar attempt at writing shorter songs was made. This baker's dozen contained a much wider range of styles, going not merely from introspective minor-key stuff to bombastic prog workouts, but also ventured into jazz, and even a relatively uncomplicated straight-up rocker.

Trisector was VdGG's final release on the Virgin label. From *A Grounding in Numbers* to the present, the band has worked exclusively with the Cherry Red label, with their albums coming out on the Esoteric Antenna subsidiary arm. *Grounding* was also the first album of new material since the 1970s to see a release in a vinyl format along with the standard CD issue. Almost exactly one month after the album was released, Cherry Red / Esoteric released a 7" vinyl single of 'Highly Strung', backed with an instrumental track titled 'Elsewhere', which would resurface again on the band's next album, *ALT*. The release was done specifically for Record Store Day and was limited to a run of 1000 copies.

'Your Time Starts Now' (Banton, Evans, Hammill)

The first song on *A Grounding in Numbers* finds the band in familiar territory. 'Your Time Starts Now' soars with a slow grace as it builds towards a Hammill-esque, pathos-filled climax. Taking its eponymous cue from the common game-show phrase, Hammill returns to a theme that he's explored many times, with varied approaches, throughout his solo career: the paradox of one's present slipping by while one tries to live a life. 'All that information / All that warp and weft / For all your patient fortitude you're patently bereft / Of clue, of hint, of notion / of answers, even vague'. In fact, this is the only 21st Century VdGG song that Hammill has performed in a solo context.

The warning that too much thinking and reflecting can, ironically, leave one ill-prepared to act in the present in any meaningful way is borne on the familiar crest of Banton's sympathetic organ tones and Evans's steady percussive coaxing. Hammill provides a piano counterpoint to the organ, as well as some poignantly colourful guitar bits in the background.

'Mathematics' (Banton, Evans, Hammill)

An oddball even by VdGG standards, this keyboard-driven paean to the amorphous titular science, takes the torch passed to it by 2008's 'Interference Patterns' and presses onward. Hammill, as lyricist, is, in his praise for and awe of the systems of numbers and equations that seem to underpin all of existence, unabashed almost to the point of silliness. Lines like 'Mathematics, just so "wow" it brooks belief', are juxtaposed with a literally sung recitation of Euler's identity. Euler was a hugely influential 18th Century mathematician, and his equation, reproduced here in the song, is known as a prime example of 'mathematical beauty', a phrase mathematicians use to describe the aesthetic pleasure that can be derived from their field of study, where it's often compared to music or poetry. Oddly, there's no metaphor at work here; the song really is about mathematics for its own sake. The music is mostly down to Banton's organ melody and embellishments, with Hammill's piano work weighing in as well. It's intriguing, and the sparkling quality of the organ tones work well with the subject matter and awestruck vibe, but it's not one of the more memorable tunes in the VdGG songbook.

'Highly Strung' (Banton, Evans, Hammill)

The third track on *A Grounding in Numbers* dispenses with the polished reserve that characterised the first two songs. 'Highly Strung' comes in fast and strong (and loud!) with a multi-tracked guitar attack from Hammill. This song is shot through with seriously thorny polyrhythms thanks to Evans's and Banton's drum and organ collisions with Hammill's guitar It's the guitar, however, that remains in the forefront throughout, and Hammill's interlocking lines provide the excess of tension that makes this song so maddeningly catchy. There are two instrumental passages where the complex interplay of strings and drums is reminiscent of King Crimson's work on their seminal *Discipline* album. Fitting music for Hammill's lyrical description of being tripped up by fight-or-flight adrenaline at a crucial moment.

'Red Baron' (Banton, Evans, Hammill)

'Highly Strung' dissolves directly into this brief instrumental that is a vehicle for Guy Evans to stretch out beyond his role as timekeeper and bring his own musical vision to fruition. With just the barest minimum of sonic textures and pulses from Banton, Evans is left, literally, to his own devices, the percussive nature of which are not limited to the normal components of a drumkit. The piece is reminiscent of Evans's work on the fourth and final volume of the *Long Hello* series of albums – a place for Van der Graaf Generator members (mostly without Hammill) to explore musical ideas without being hemmed in by VdGG constraints.

'Bunsho' (Banton, Evans, Hammill)

'Bunsho' is one of the few tracks on *A Grounding in Numbers* that comes close to 'epic' territory, with a riff for the ages. Starting off with a gently rolling guitar/vocal introduction, the proceedings quickly become heavy with aggressive organ work and drumming. As the vocals heat up, Hammill's guitar meshes menacingly with Banton's playing, creating a juggernaut propelled by Evans's strident drumming. The riff is deliberate, inexorable, and very, very satisfying. Of course, like any song with a riff this good cannot help but end too soon; after the trio builds to and briefly sustains the climax, the tension abruptly drops off, and Hammill quickly finishes the song in the manner in which it began.

Lyrically, 'Bunsho' reads like a cautionary fable, using irony to drive home the point that the value and importance one ascribes to things they create are not necessarily matched by those who stand to judge the creations. According to Banton, the story of 'Bunsho' is one that Hammill encountered in classic Japanese literature, and to which he related.

'Snake Oil' (Banton, Evans, Hammill)

The second of two back to back mini-epics, 'Snake Oil' is nevertheless quite different in character from 'Bunsho'. The song takes off at a fairly brisk speed, with Hammill on piano this time, and Banton producing overlaid organ parts with a myriad of different effects. The band chugs along like a cartoon train with Hammill hanging out front, rapidly throwing out lyrics like tracks in front of the car in order to avoid derailment.

A middle section slows the tempo, and the music takes a dark, mechanical turn, giving the impression of entering a tunnel. The lyrics, which are concerned with the extreme cognitive dissonance displayed by devotees of certain spiritual gurus or political ideologues, here focus on the inner workings of these personality-cults. The lyrics are almost distressingly contemporary, and, much like those of 'Every Bloody Emperor' from the previous decade, only seem to become more pertinent and pointed as time goes on.

'Splink' (Banton, Evans, Hammill)

Just as 'Red Baron' provided a sort of palate cleanser between the first three songs on 'Grounding' and what came next, so does 'Splink' serve as an intermission between the second and third act. This is a light-hearted and quirky instrumental, featuring Peter Hammill on a quirky fretless electric bass, known as an 'Ashbury', as well as guitar. As Banton recalls, the Ashbury didn't cover the actual bass lines; those were played by him, on a Fender. Banton also was responsible for all the keyboard parts, including harpsichord!

It's a very evocative piece that the instruments seem to want to take in different directions at once. The title comes from public service announcements that ran in the 1970s on British television – 'SPLINK' was a mnemonic used to teach and remind children how to safely cross busy intersections. The spot was lampooned for its needlessly confusing and overly wordy approach, and this tune playfully mirrors the confusion that it engendered. Notably, the PSA's talking head was the actor Jon Pertwee, who played the third 'Doctor Who' in the long-running eponymous television series.

'Embarrassing Kid' (Banton, Evans, Hammill)

This next section of *A Grounding in Numbers* kicks off with a growl. 'Embarrassing Kid' is nothing new in terms of lyrical themes, but, musically, it's a complete departure for the band. With a snarling guitar tone and strident playing, Hammill, as an ageing Rikki Nadir, leads the trio in a hard-rocking coming-to-terms with mistakes made by a youthful self. It's a short burst of 'alternate universe' VdGG, ironic in that the band already seems to have arrived from another dimension!

'Medusa' (Banton, Evans, Hammill)

The shortest track on *A Grounding in Numbers* isn't one of the instrumental nuggets, as one might expect, but a fully formed song. 'Medusa' is simple in terms of structure, but complicated by the number of overlapping instruments. Hammill's sour-toned guitar brings to mind the introduction to The Animals' 'House of the Rising Sun' taken to its basics as he begins the song. After one bar, Evans joins in on drums. Banton is late to the party, but more than makes up for it with his contributions on bass guitar, organ, and harpsichord. As this brief excursion into the danger implied by the title, Hammill repeats the darkly and wryly humorous refrain, in the voice of the eponymous character, 'What you see is what you get from me', while Banton continues to open up what began as a very compressed and claustrophobic sound field. While the harpsichord is an entirely new wrinkle in the VdGG canon, the organ trills sound like they could have come directly from the *World Record* sessions 35 years prior.

'Mr. Sands' (Banton, Evans, Hammill)

There is no break between 'Medusa' and 'Mr. Sands'; Banton's flurry of ascending organ notes that close the previous track can be heard continuing their upwards and outwards arc at the beginning of this song. As the organ notes continue their fade-out, a chorus of Hammill 'ooh' bring the new tune in (organ again in the lead). Banton does a lot of the work here – the organ provides the lead as well as atmospheric embellishments, and the bass pedals work with Evans's percussion, in overdrive on this track, to provide the rhythm section. Hammill, as he did on 'Snake Oil', ploughs forward on piano and gives voice to the dense lyrics.

'Mr. Sands' is certainly one of the most ambitious, and successful, pieces on 'A Grounding in Numbers'. The catchiness of the tune and the mounting intensity both accurately reflect the lyrical concern; the growing awareness that disaster is going to strike in a crowded theatre, as a metaphor for our inability to read existential warning signs until it's too late – 'Everything's in code / Till the moment it explodes'. 'Mr. Sands' is a catchword used by employees working in heavily populated public areas to communicate the presence of danger to colleagues without alarming the crowd.

'Smoke' (Banton, Evans, Hammill)

Appropriately, a song featuring the troublesome 'Mr. Sands' leads into 'Smoke', which has a similar lyrical theme, although approached much more elliptically. It's another very short song, but very busy, and another strange excursion for the trio. The tune slinks erratically but confidently through a dense sound field. A single note is played eight times before a bass guitar kicks in, as well as the spoken voices of the three band members, audible but impossible to understand. This is followed by a mélange of other instruments: drums, keyboards, and even Banton on guitar. The result is an odd swirl of post-punk, funk, rock, and jazz, but it's ultimately uncategorisable, though absolutely enjoyable. Hammill modulates his voice and makes it waver in mock-trepidation, tossing out lines like, 'Just be careful of where your mouse clicks'. Both this song and 'Mr. Sands' seem to share a thematic kinship with 'Splink' – pitting caution against confusion and panic.

'5533' (Banton, Evans, Hammill)

Another quirky song, '5533' sees Banton handing off guitar duties to Guy Evans. For its two and a half minutes, the song channels a classic sci-fi movie laboratory come to life as an archetypal mad scientist wheels about the room rattling off truths that are at once obscurely arcane and terribly prescient. The music is at the outer reaches of Van der Graafian chaos – the guitars, the gleefully meandering bass, and the numerous layers of keyboards, each doing their own thing, barely hang together, and Hammill's off-kilter declamations further complicate the situation, but it is a glorious mess. One gets the feeling that it all actually fits together quite well on some cosmic level that is unfathomable to the listener but nonetheless mathematically sound.

It is harder than usual to follow what Hammill is singing about, but the half-sung, half-spoken titular refrain hearkens back to 'Mathematics'. Leonhard Euler, of the 'identity' that's rhapsodised about in the second track, was a pioneer in mathematical approaches to music. He found that octaves could be divided with prime numbers, specifically 3 and 5. On a lighter, comically self-referential note, '5533' also refers to the very time signature of what's being played while the number is being sung – 5/4, 5/4. 3/4, 3/4.

'All Over the Place' (Banton, Evans, Hammill)
The album ends on a note that can really only be described as 'classic VdGG'. There are a few references to other catalogue highlights, but, taken as a whole, this song sounds unlike anything the band has attempted. The track can be divided into four parts: the first is a lengthy introduction, followed by an explosive segue into the main riff, then a sombre and becalmed digression, before leaning into the main riff once more, with phasers set to kill.

The song begins with Hammill and Banton playing insistent and almost identical riffs; the former on piano, and the latter on harpsichord. Evans provides a minimal beat on bass drum, and Hammill sings two verses, setting the lyrical scene. Musically, the song stands alone, but lyrically it's very much of a piece with other Hammill lyrics from VdGG as well as solo work ('Masks' comes to mind, as does 'Sharply Unclear' from the 1994 solo Hammill album *Roaring Forties*). The lyrics describe a man who's become dissatisfied and disillusioned with his social life to the point of abandoning it for a more interior one, presumably on social media.

When the song's main riff kicks in, the piano and harpsichord are joined by organ and Evans's full drumkit. Banton's harpsichord playing retreats to a spot on the right side of the stereo field, playing at about the same speed as before, while the other keyboards lumber forward methodically but forcefully. Hammill shifts to describing, with a lead vocal and a chorus of backing vocals – singing lines not reflected in the printed lyrics – what happened to the man's psyche as he found himself living performatively for an online audience.

What follows this part of the song is an extended soliloquy played in a minor key, fleshing out a brief hint of a melody introduced at the end of the first part of the song. The point of view changes from the second to the first person, and Hammill's narrator attempts to put his feelings of estrangement into words. As the lyrical image dissolves, the main riff is reprised, without vocals, but with even more instrumental muscle – 'bashing' comes to mind, as well as the closing section of a Van der Graaf Generator song from some forty years prior: 'White Hammer'.

ALT (2012)

Personnel:
Hugh Banton: organ, bass
Guy Evans: drums, percussion, field recording
Peter Hammill: guitar, piano
Produced at The Gaia Centre, Terra Incognita, The Organ Workshop, 2006-2012 by
Van der Graaf Generator.
UK release date and label: June 2012; Esoteric.
Running time: 1:01:01

After two consecutive three-year gaps between releasing new material, Van der Graaf Generator delivered a new album only 15 months after *A Grounding in Numbers* was sent forth into the world. The new album, *ALT*, was in danger of being overshadowed by other goings-on: Peter Hammill had just released a solo album, *Consequences*, and VdGG had just embarked on a highly-publicised North American tour. But *ALT* was never intended as a front-line full-on proper VdGG album. It carries the descriptor, on the back cover underneath the title, 'Instrumental Improvs & Experiments'.

The recordings contained on *ALT* are indeed from an alternate VdGG world, where traditional (even for this band) song structures are set aside in favour of mostly non-linear and exploratory sound sculptures. The album is comprised of recordings made during rehearsals and recording sessions dating back to the first time the band had gathered as a trio, in 2006, to sessions that occurred just prior to the completion of *A Grounding in Numbers*. As Hammill has noted, this collection is not without precedence. It stands as a complement to the second disc in 2005's *Present* release, although those improvisations belonged to one small burst of rehearsals and weren't given the time and space to breathe and steep in the band's collective consciousness that the material on *ALT* enjoyed.

But there are other precedents as well: the duo improv album that Evans and Hammill released in 1988, *Spur of the Moment*, Hammill's solo documentations of sonic experiments ranging from the early 1980s (*Loops & Reels*) to the early 2000s (*Unsung*), Evans's work with the experimental musical collective Echo City, and even the experimental VdGG recordings made during the early 1970s hiatus and compiled on *Time Vaults*. This is, however, the first completely intentional VdGG release of a collection of experimental instrumentals.

ALT was released on the Cherry Red / Esoteric label in CD and vinyl editions. The latter is a heavily abbreviated version of the CD, containing only 8 of the 14 tracks, but it includes one short piece which doesn't appear on the CD. The very entertaining liner notes were supplied by Guy Evans.

'Earlybird' (Banton, Evans, Hammill)

There's no easing into the strangeness of this album, which is kicked off with an immersive sound world of birdcalls and insistent but unobtrusive percussion. Evans toils away on the cymbals, as well as other percussive instruments that produce lush, resonant sounds. In fact, according to Hugh Banton, this track was entirely conceived and realised by Evans! Indeed, the sonics here are so rich and enveloping that a listener might feel as if an airlock has sealed behind them. Sudden barometric change: strange humidity.

This particular track enjoyed a life after the release of *ALT*. Vladislav Shabalin, a Russian environmental artist, based in Italy, who works with fossils, was a long-time VdGG fan and was inspired by 'Earlybird' to create an installation consisting of trees and birdhouses made out of petrified wood. Speakers, playing 'Earlybird', would be installed inside the birdhouses. Shabalin approached VdGG with the idea in 2013, and the band agreed to attach their name and publicly endorse Shabalin's installation, the 'Earlybird Project', which toured the world from 2013 to 2017.

'Extractus' (Banton, Evans, Hammill)

This is an extremely short piece that sounds as if it might have been recorded in preparation for 'The Hurlyburly' on *Trisector*. Evans is strong out of the gate with a loud and strident drum rolls while Hammill gallops along on guitar, alternating fast-picked lines with hesitant sustained two-note phrases. Eventually, he switches gears and opts for arpeggiated note-clusters, but Evans never deviates from his pattern. Towards the end, Banton provides an ambient tone in the background that comes forward at the end as a pulsating drone. Possibly as close to 'rock' as *ALT* gets, 'Extractus' is a mixture of velocity and longing.

'Sackbutt' (Banton, Evans, Hammill)

This is another drum workout, with mournful ersatz bagpipes sounding off. The piece has a rustic quality; there are lots of low rumblings coming from the depths of the objects that Evans is hitting (he goes far beyond a standard drumkit here). The organ-sourced bagpipe begins to recede as a heavily treated guitar rises to the foreground, initially sounding quite similar to the ersatz bagpipes, but quickly entering into harsher sonic territory. Towards the end of this short piece, the organ returns to share the stage while Evans slows his pace, resulting in an atmospheric aural snapshot of a possibly medieval scene.

'Colossus' (Banton, Evans, Hammill)

The previous two tracks, both under two minutes, are followed by 'Colossus', a substantially longer piece which, at six minutes, gives the band some time to develop a theme. The theme here is reminiscent of the thrill of an amusement park madhouse. Banton, who is in overdrive on this track, assaults the senses like the soundtrack to a 3D-surround film of an astral rollercoaster ride. Evans, who has been in strong form so far on *ALT*, picks up the gauntlet towards the end of 'Colossus', matching Banton's wild energy with his own.

The tune also features a lot of faux-reed instrument sounds (first woodwind and then brass) from Banton's organ – perhaps in homage (or something less kind?) to David Jackson? Or a conciliatory gesture to fans who have bemoaned this loss? Maybe even a display of darkly ironic musical commentary. What can be said with certainty, is that 'Colossus' is a demented but absolutely engaging work, and it ably refutes the argument that the lack of 'normal' song structures somehow relegates 'ALT' to a second-tier release.

'Batty Loop' (Banton, Evans, Hammill)

As the title implies, there are two keyboard parts, presumably from Hammill, that are looped and played back at different volumes and speeds, over the top of cymbal work from Evans. The keyboard riffs are appealingly catchy, but at just over one minute in length, there's not really enough time for them to really catch hold, let alone develop.

'Splendid' (Banton, Evans, Hammill)

Of all the tracks on *ALT*, this one sounds the most like one of the improv jams from the second disc of *Present*, and it is particularly reminiscent of Banton's 1970s organ sound. This is gleefully earthy prog – you can see the smiles on the trio's faces. It's also hard to get a handle on what exactly you're hearing. Guy Evans is drumming furiously underneath what seems like two organs – one, loud in the foreground, sounds like a Hammond B3 and is played with floor-shaking intensity and volume; the other hangs in the background and adds depth to the sonic palette. At about two-thirds of the way in, Hammill joins in on guitar. It's a monstrously heavy, and quite fun, slice of improvised prog/blues rock. As the unnamed speaker says at the end of the track, 'Splendid!'

'Repeat After Me' (Banton, Evans, Hammill)

This is another relatively straightforward improvisation, stretched out to twice the length of the previous track. Much calmer and more restrained than 'Splendid', 'Repeat After Me' is primarily a duet. Banton turns in an exquisite performance on electric bass, and Hammill plays electric piano, with a sound and style that hearkens back to his mid-late 1980s work. Evans gamely joins in on drums about halfway through, but this is Banton's and Hammill's show.

'Elsewhere' (Banton, Evans, Hammill)

This track was originally released as the B-side to the 'Highly Strung' single in 2011; it appears here unaltered. 'Elsewhere' is extremely spacey; this track could have fit in well as an intermission during 'Pioneers Over c'. There are two keyboards and a ton of effects, which could come from either Hammill or Banton. Almost certainly, Hammill is once again playing electric piano, with Banton on organ. What is abundantly clear, however, is that Evans is attacking the drums like a demon. Despite the cosmic tones, the band lurches into a syncopated jazz rhythm, and it all starts to sound a little Sun Ra. Before long, though, it all dissolves into a haze of sonics.

'Here's One I Made Earlier' (Banton, Evans, Hammill)

VdGG does an excellent imitation of Fripp and Eno here: the track sounds uncannily similar to something off of their albums *No Pussyfooting* or *Evening Star*. Soft clacking sounds, looped, recur at steady intervals. Hammill, with heavily processed guitar, solos twice throughout the track. The first is relatively unassuming, but the second, at about four minutes, carries a good deal more punch. Both sound like Fripp's guitar work from the above-mentioned albums. As Fripp played material from the *No Pussyfooting* album before King Crimson performances in 1973, so too did VdGG use this track, as well as 'Repeat After Me', as pre-show music on their first tours in the trio format.

'Midnite Or So' (Banton, Evans, Hammill)

As the title playfully indicates, this is a slow-burning ode to John Barry's 'Theme From *Midnight Cowboy*'. Banton ably and lovingly apes Toots Thielemans's harmonica sound with his organ; Hammill, on piano, and Evans flesh out the ad hoc jazz combo. At the end of the track, Banton employs the same nose-dive effect that can be heard on the introduction to 'Your Time Starts Now'.

'D'Accord' (Banton, Evans, Hammill)

This is a subtle, ghostly piece that never really rises out of the shadows. Banton and Hammill, on organ and keyboards, swirl around each other in a fog of echoes and reverb. 'D'Accord' needs to be turned way up, headphones utilised, to really grasp the nuances, like the very minimal guitar notes plucked toward the end.

'Mackerel Ate Them' (Banton, Evans, Hammill)

Another live power-trio jam. Banton makes with the weird organ sounds, Evans drums reliably, and Hammill gives the whammy bar on his guitar a solid and thorough workout. At times it's hard to distinguish what Hammill is doing on guitar from keyboard effects, but when he hits the bar, it becomes apparent. Halfway through the track, Evans inexplicably drops off the map, and Hammill and Banton remain, keepers of the gallery of deranged sound effects. Evans returns after a spell, though, and carries the improvised tune home. Hammill's thrust-and-parry approach, particularly before the break, is very similar to his playing during the introduction to the trio's live rendition of 'Lemmings'.

'Tuesday, the Riff' (Banton, Evans, Hammill)

Tuesday or not, this is the most 'songlike' of anything on *ALT*; it sounds ready for vocals to be laid over the top. The trio (drums, organ, guitar) have whipped up what could be the theme song in a soundtrack for a thriller/horror movie. Banton keeps the tension ratcheted up to ten throughout the entire three-minute piece, sending off alarm sounds as the track ends, while Hammill puts forth a subtly menacing, minimalist, guitar part. Evans's drumming is equally restrained; few flourishes, all in service to the riff.

'Dronus' (Banton, Evans, Hammill)

The final track on *ALT* is also the third 'us' piece (preceded by 'Extractus' and 'Colossus'). Clocking in at over ten minutes, it has plenty of time to unfold, and it does so quite slowly, rather drone-like, as the title implies. 'Dronus' is hardly placid, though; it's full of a restlessness that's different in character from the rest of the more gregarious tracks on the album. The organ and keyboard effects ebb and flow, at times with a studied languor, at others, obliquely menacing. For Hammill's part, it sounds like he's referencing his late 1990s work, particularly the quasi-ambient long-form piece, 'The Light Continent' on his 1998 album, *This*. Banton seems to be cribbing slightly from his *Pawn Hearts*-era 'Diminutions' solo effort. 'Dronus' has very little in common with the other tracks on *ALT*, at least on the surface; but on further reflection, it shows itself to be another way in which the trio bring their storehouses of musical experience together as pioneers, in a new, unsettled and unsettling, land.

Do Not Disturb (2016)

Personnel:
Hugh Banton: organ, keyboards, bass guitar, accordion, glockenspiel
Guy Evans: drums, percussion
Peter Hammill: vocals, piano, guitar
Produced at Stage 2 Studios, Bath, October 2015 by Van der Graaf Generator
UK release date and label: September 2016; Esoteric
Highest chart places: UK: 88 Netherlands: 96
Running time: 57:07

In 2016, Van der Graaf Generator released *Do Not Disturb*, the last album of new material to be released under that name at the time of this book's publication. The band has said that the possibility that it might be the final album was on all of their minds during the writing and recording process, while noting that it wasn't a done deal. In any case, it certainly informed the substance of the album. The previous albums all contained a fair number of lyrics centred on the prospect of ageing, but there, VdGG seemed more like relatively disinterested observers. With *Do Not Disturb*, it felt like these concerns may have materialised as an impasse rather than just an eyebrow-raiser.

If it turns out to be VdGG's final statement, it will have ended their recorded run with a howl, not a whimper, into the abyss. Hammill, never one for rating his own or VdGG's work, has said that he thinks that 'it's the best work that we've done in the modern era of the group'. It does have a greater degree of that patently ineffable Van der Graaf Generator spirit than any of the three prior studio albums; there's an alchemically potent mix of cerebral complexity, emotional directness, and fearless going-for-it that runs through *Do Not Disturb* rather more consistently than in many of their albums. Most of the songs also contain a number of changes, giving them more of a kinship to the 20th Century VdGG repertoire than anything recorded this century.

For the recording of this album, the trio decided to retain control over all aspects of production. Thus, the sound doesn't have the same brightness or sheen that was present on *A Grounding in Numbers*, but it still plays to the band's strengths. While the sonics may not be crystal clear, they are nonetheless able to relay the magical interplay of musical ideas that makes Van der Graaf Generator so inimitable and unique. The band also, for the first time, committed to fully rehearsing each song before going into the studio to record. The instrumentation on this album isn't quite as varied as it was on *Grounding*; it's worth noting, however, that Banton brings another new instrument into the VdGG world for the first time: the accordion!

'Aloft' (Banton, Evans, Hammill)
The first part of the song comes in like a breeze, with Hammill's guitar chords wafting to the foreground. The drums are hit lightly and sparingly, and

Banton's bass guitar pulses rapidly on the ground, keeping the tune from drifting into the atmosphere, where organ tones shimmer ever so faintly. The vocals complement the music thus far – breathy and buoyant in cadence, earthy in tone.

The second part of the song comes in at about two and a half minutes, and here Banton takes the lead on organ, accompanying himself on accordion. It's quite a bit more driven than the opening section, and leads directly into the steam-powered high point of the song, bringing Hammill, his guitar sounding much more assertive, to the front once again, in step with Banton, as the vocals become scathing and urgent in tone. This section of the song bears strong resemblance to the equivalent portion of a similarly tiered solo song of Hammill's from almost twenty years before – 'Unrehearsed', the lead track from his album *This*.

Following the song's early adrenaline payoff, the earlier themes are revisited in reverse order, taking the band, and the listener, back to the start. Lyrically, the song is a pastiche of numerous earlier Hammill songs, most notably 'Flight', which not only shares a conceptual similarity with 'Aloft', but also a kinship in central metaphor; in the earlier song, the protagonist pilots a plane, and in the current selection, the anti-hero is an aeronaut, guiding or being carried away by a hot-air balloon. The latter vehicle is a particularly apt choice for this set of lyrics since the character being addressed in second-person finds himself in trouble as a result of the hot air of his verbal bravado turning against him.

'Alfa Berlina' (Banton, Evans, Hammill)

While it's safe to say that most Van der Graaf Generator lyrics contain an element of biographical material embedded within, 'Alfa Berlina' is the rare specimen that is taken directly from the collective VdGG diary. In Italy, during the tour following the release of *Pawn Hearts*, the band were driven from town to town by the promoter at dangerously high speeds in his Alfa Romeo. It was at this point that the band came as close as they ever would to approaching a 'rock star' level of fame; their new album was at the top of the Italian charts, and VdGG concerts were mobbed to the point of being flashpoints for political extremism.

Thus, 'Alfa Berlina' (a type of Alfa Romeo) is an evocative distillation of their Italian experience, compressing everything into a snapshot. Such compression leads to the events described in the song acquiring an aura of cosmic significance: 'I saw a wolf high upon the mountain pass / The stars were tumbling end to end...'. It follows 'Aloft' as a song involving a very different kind of vehicle, and to denote that musical difference, the band adapts accordingly. The introductory lyrical preamble is accompanied by Hammill's guitar effects and – in a rare move for VdGG – by external field recordings of traffic noise. Shouts and sirens underpin Hammill's 'come back with me to a simpler time' offer.

The bulk of the song is organ-driven, with workmanlike drumming from Evans, and Hammill's guitar continuing to provide motor-like effects as well as added muscle to Banton's organ work. Aside from the intro and the interlude, this is probably as straight-ahead mid-tempo rock and roll as VdGG get. The interlude, though, is VdGG at the other end of the spectrum, building eerie scaffolding on which to position a makeshift visionary experience. Organ and guitar effects abound, buoying Hammill's mystical, trance-like retelling of a vision he'd had from the back seat of the car that hurtled through a foreign country in a time lost to memory.

'Room 1210' (Banton, Evans, Hammill)

This song has quite a lot in common with 'The Final Reel', from the *Trisector* album. The lyrics once again investigate the liminal space between life and death, this time from the point of view of a person seemingly eager to check out, as it were. Musically, as well, 'Room 1210' is a mournful, piano-heavy song, but with more stops and starts, and changes, than its predecessor.

The song opens with Hammill alone on vocals and piano, and is shortly accompanied by Banton on accordion. Bass and drums soon follow, but barely get started before the song abruptly shifts to a complex and intricate organ riff, behind which can be heard two guitar tracks – one playing a version of the organ riff, and the other a backwards-recorded solo that sounds like communication attempts from a party of ghosts. And they get at the heart of the song, which is an acknowledgement of the existence of spirits in the eponymous hotel room, whom the protagonist is resigned, perhaps even eager, to join. (The title of the album, in fact, comes from the protagonist's plea to those on the other side of the hotel room door: 'do not disturb him any more'.)

The intricacy of the riff morphs into a looser, more powerful one that's bashed out very satisfyingly with all hands on deck – piano, organ, guitar, bass, and drums. After a time, the piano/accordion/bass/drums section so abruptly abandoned is resumed, and the song's final three minutes finish out with languorous playing, of which the accordion remains a highlight, melding surprisingly effectively with the well-established VdGG sound.

'Forever Falling' (Banton, Evans, Hammill)

It's astounding how much the trio was able to pack into this relatively short song. As 'Room 1210' was a sort of extension of 'The Final Reel', so does 'Forever Falling' seem to channel and expand upon the hyper-pop characteristics of the earlier 'Highly Strung'. All three players are out in the foreground: burbling organ, strutting guitar, and drums that snake through and surround the entire event. Hammill is at his best here, lyrically and vocally. The writing displays a remarkable attention to detail as well as the larger philosophical implications of the situation described therein, and his delivery is brightly and cleanly rendered, highlighting the nuances of his uniquely weathered voice without letting those features get in their own way.

Three verses in and the high-octane fuel comes out, in a transitional chorus-like section that ratchets up the tension and leads to the middle portion of the song, where ebullience mixes with a devilishly tricky mess of time signatures, for what's probably the most deliriously upbeat romp VdGG has ever engaged in. A false feint to the opening theme comes next, before a lateral jump into yet another completely new section. Finally, there is a return to the verse/chorus opening part of the song, with an additional fury held over from the middle of the song.

'Shikata Ga Nai' (Banton)

This is a brief and gentle instrumental from Hugh Banton. According to Hammill, it was brought to the table well after the other recordings (except for 'Go') were completed, and the foundation was already laid by Banton with organ and accordion, needing only some percussion flourishes to be overdubbed by Evans. Cinematic, and with a distinctively European flavour, it could easily have fit in with the material on *ALT*, although it obviously wasn't at all experimental.

'(Oh No I Must Have Said) Yes' (Banton, Evans, Hammill)

Of course, a delicate instrumental piece can only be followed, in perverse Van der Graaf logic, by a monolithic beast of a rocker. '(Oh No I Must Have Said) Yes' is a stripped-down affair, with just guitar, bass, and drums. For the first two minutes, the band thrashes out a tight riff that's repeated with manic intensity, always just this side of going completely off the rails, as Hammill belts out a wry lyric that bemusedly attempts to come to terms with the long tail of personal responsibility.

The middle four minutes of this long song ramps up the already electric tension that Evans, Banton, and Hammill have achieved while turning the volume way down. Hammill's crushing guitar now sounds tentative as it picks its way through the web of bass notes that Banton lays down. Similarly, Evans turns from skin bashing to daintily resonant metal taps. Very slowly, the trio builds back up to the juggernaut that they abandoned, and rampage on to the end of the song. There's nothing halfway about this one; that it was pulled off implies a hard-won level of confidence that the trio has in themselves, each other, and the group as a unit.

'Brought to Book' (Banton, Evans, Hammill)

If *Do Not Disturb* is indeed the final Van der Graaf Generator album, then the band have acquitted themselves well with the last three songs. 'Brought to Book' marries the bracing intensity of VdGG's early work with the playful finesse of their more recent material. The lyrical theme of coming to terms with past missteps, is, by now, quite familiar – another facet of the same crystal.

'Brought to Book' begins with a modern jazz feel, as the band sets out in search of the song, with piano, bass, and drums. Before long, the pace picks up and Banton takes over with a bracing organ riff. When the song reverts back to the piano trio format, the slightly sour tone of Hammill's guitar joins the ensemble, for a much briefer stint before heading off again into parts unknown.

This time organ and guitar trade-off and overlap each other with parts of the same riff, while Evans beats out a daunting path on the drums. A false wrap-up is next, with heroic guitar licks and 'farewell-to-everyone' epic-ending vocals, but the trio has other plans, and gleefully pulls the rug out from under the listener – VdGG is not done yet. The electric riff returns, more frantic as if the band is feeling the pressure of trying to do what needs to be done as the sand piles up at the bottom of the hourglass. Except that they sound like they're having a blast. The band finally reaches a more fitting ending marked by a sense of incompletion, as though there's still something more to be found – the only honest way to end.

'Almost the Words' (Banton, Evans, Hammill)

Starting out in a similar fashion to 'Brought to Book', with a jazz-ish piano/drums/bass combo, 'Almost the Words' distinguishes itself from its disc-mate by the restless drive towards some resolution. Hammill's vocals add a degree of impatience that pushes the band's playing away from anything resembling complacency. Nevertheless, the instrumentation remains the same for a much longer period of time than the previous track, building tension organically rather than jumping to different sonic thresholds.

The payoff, when the inevitable change finally does come, is immense. At just over the song's halfway point, after Hammill's considerable feats of wordplay have been exhausted, Banton takes over keyboard duties, and the abrupt shift brings us all the way back to 'Pawn Hearts', as he and Evans recreate the instrumental madness that was the 'Kosmos Tours' section of 'A Plague of Lighthouse-Keepers'! Hammill ups the spine-tingle ante with a carefully sculpted choir of his own voice, half-singing / half-declaiming the final four lines of the lyric. Almost two minutes into this section, you begin to hear another sound world demanding entry from the wings, and the keyboard/drums polyphony gives way to a good old-fashioned guitar/organ/drums free-for-all, and VdGG exits the stage the way that it should – in an electrostatic cloud of glorious noise.

'Go' (Banton, Evans, Hammill)

The true closer of the album, however, is 'Go'. Minimalist in title and content, this song is another departure for the band. Virtually a duet between Banton on the organ and Hammill on vocals, Evans and Hammill provide only the tiniest of instrumental colour, with a brief cymbal flourish and a single guitar effect. Long-time fans will note a resemblance to the 1976 title track on the *Still Life* album, but 'Go', to this author's ears, is a devastatingly personal hymn to past and future selves, at once explanation and admonishment.

The vinyl edition of *Do Not Disturb*, released concurrently with the CD, does not contain all of the songs listed above, and the remaining tracks are presented in a different, less sensible, order:

Side A
'Aloft'
'Brought to Book'
'(Oh No I Must Have Said) Yes'

Side B
'Alfa Berlina'
'Room 1210'
'Almost the Words'
'Go'

Et Cetera
Time Vaults (1982)
Personnel:
Hugh Banton: organ, bass
Guy Evans: drums
Peter Hammill: vocals, guitar, piano, bass
David Jackson: saxophone, piano
Chris Judge Smith: vocals
Produced at Sofa Sound, 1981, by Peter Hammill
UK release date and label: 1982, Sofa Sound. US release date and label: November 2008; Abstract Sounds
Running time: 45:18

In 1981, Peter Hammill compiled and released this collection of 'lost' Van der Graaf Generator recordings that were made during the post-*Pawn Hearts* and pre-*Godbluff* hiatus. Barring a few vocal overdubs from Hammill and a saxophone overdub from David Jackson, these tracks were taken directly from the original tapes and only marginally cleaned up by Hammill in his Sofa Sound studio. The three tracks that contain vocals, then, have Hammill singing in 1981 over the 1971-75 instrumentals.

These recordings are fairly rough, certainly not what one might consider to be 'studio quality'. *Time Vaults*, Hammill wrote in the liner notes, is an 'anti-compilation … intended for those who are already VdGG aficionados!' The songs range in states of completion from rudimentary demos to reasonably finished songs. It's far from easy listening, but a fascinating look into what the band was doing in the early 1970s.

Time Vaults has had something of a chequered history, in terms of pressings and releases. Originally self-released by Hammill on cassette in 1981, it was issued as an LP in Brazil, Portugal, and the United Kingdom in 1985. As audio technology advanced, the album enjoyed another release on CD in 1992 in the UK, 1994 in France, and the United States in 2008. Oddly, the US reissue does away with Hammill's original liner notes, replacing them with pointless and largely uninformed verbiage that occasionally paraphrases Hammill's commentary.

To complicate matters further, a VdGG compilation album titled *Now and Then* was released in the UK in 1987 and reissued several times over the years, with the latest re-release in 2009. It contains two songs from *Time Vaults* ('The Liquidator' and 'Tarzan') and six songs from an album released by Jackson / Banton / Evans in 1985, *Gentlemen Prefer Blues*. *Now and Then* was never authorised by Van der Graaf Generator.

'The Liquidator' (Hammill)
The backing track to this fantastic lost song was recorded in Autumn, 1973 along with the bulk of the material that comprised *The Silent Corner and*

the Empty Stage. It shares certain stylistic traits with 'Forsaken Gardens' from that album, but while the album track switches from slow to fast tempo several times, 'Liquidator' is played at a uniform speed (after the long introduction), with an unflagging energy. The instrumental breakouts of the two songs nevertheless sound remarkably similar. David Jackson's saxophone careens over the rest of the instruments on display: Hammill's galloping piano, Hugh Banton's bass and organ, and some thunderous drums from Guy Evans.

Hammill's lyrics, sung almost ten years after they were written, are humorous and poignant in their self-reflexive (at the band level) stock-taking: 'I read the news in a paper: no flowers, please, donations to charity like the N.S.P.C.V.d.G.G. – yeah, send the money to Guy and Hugh and David and me'. The song is perhaps something of an explanatory note to fans who weren't in the loop (this was of course long before the internet) as to why VdGG folded. It's a cruel irony that this gem of a Van der Graaf Generator song, by definition, couldn't have appeared on a contemporaneous VdGG album.

'Rift Valley' (Hammill, Jackson, Evans)

During the studio rehearsals for the *Godbluff* album in early 1975, when Hugh Banton was often apart from the rest of the band, trying to upgrade his organ in time for the album to be recorded, Evans, Hammill, and Jackson put together and recorded demos for two new songs. One of these was 'Rift Valley' – again, the vocals were added in Hammill's home studio in 1981. It's a hard-edged, take-no-prisoners sax/drums/electric guitar onslaught, and its unvarnished rawness only adds to its power.

The middle section of 'Rift Valley' contains a riff that would be lifted and placed, sans vocals, into 'Meurglys III' a year down the road, but here, it provides a thorny backdrop to Hammill's dense lyrics, which imagine the thoughts of the 'first man' somehow looking ahead to the future of humanity. Hammill's vocal performance throughout the song recalls the off-kilter and meandering phrasing that helped to make 'Lemmings' so unique.

'Tarzan' (Banton, Evans, Hammill, Jackson)

This is the only track on *Time Vaults* to come from the *Nadir's Big Chance* sessions at Rockfield Studios in 1974. It captures the 'Nadir' spirit quite nicely. All four VdGG members are credited with the writing of 'Tarzan', which is a very short, light-hearted instrumental. Banton plays a particularly low and lumbering bass line, over which Evans, Hammill (on electric piano), and Jackson hold forth. Before long, rain forest sound effects begin to rise in the background, and all instruments save Banton's bass fall away, and at the very end, the signature yell of the eponymous Lord of the Jungle is channelled through Jackson's saxophone, removing any doubt regarding VdGG's familiarity with pop culture!

'Coil Night' (Jackson)

The second 'Time Vaults' track to emerge from the 1975 *Godbluff* sessions, 'Coil Night' was written by David Jackson, who also provided saxophone overdubs to the recording in 1981. Jackson does double duty here, on saxophone and piano, while Hammill, unusually, plays bass. The recording levels seem to be quite 'hot', with Evans's drumming in particular leaning towards distortion, but the overdrive is very much in keeping with the Van der Graaf aesthetic. As in 'Rift Valley', Banton is notable in his absence.

'Time Vaults' (n/a)

The title track is impossible to pin down to one date or location; it's an amalgam of recordings from different sources during the 1971-75 time period, edited together by Hammill with a bizarre intuitive logic. There are quite a few bits of unidentifiable playing, as well as audio verité clips of conversations, but there are also snippets of VdGG renditions of the controversial Gainsbourg/ Birkin classic 'Je t'aime... Moi Non Plus' and 'Wunderbar' from the Cole Porter musical *Kiss Me Kate*. Also woven throughout the sonic tapestry are pieces of Van der Graaf's disarming self-parody of a BBC Peel Session, 'An Epidemic of Father Christmases', recorded in December 1971, and never commercially released. This session featured David Jackson playing the melody to 'Rudolph, the Red-Nosed Reindeer' as well as Chris Judge Smith, returning for the occasion, singing a song he'd written with Hammill in the early VdGG days, 'Christmas Can Be Terrible'. This, then, is the height of the anti-compilation, almost sure to win over no new fans, but a delight for the already converted.

'Drift (I Hope It Won't)' (Banton)

The album's title track drifts (pardon the pun) almost imperceptibly into this track, credited to Hugh Banton. 'Drift' is bookended by long stretches of semi-audible conversation punctuated by instrumental noises from members of the band. Any actual musical content is limited to about a minute in the centre of this almost three-minute track. The tune, such as it is, is played by Banton (organ), Jackson (sax), and Evans (drums); Hammill appears to sit this one out. It was recorded in July 1972, when the band were preparing to record the next album after *Pawn Hearts*, right before the break-up.

'Roncevaux' (Hammill)

This was also recorded at the July 1972 session, and would likely have featured prominently on the next VdGG album, were there in fact going to be one. Unlike the majority of the songs on *Time Vaults*, 'Roncevaux' was performed live at least once, directly after this recording was made, on 1 August, 1972 at a club in Italy.

'Roncevaux' has all the hallmarks of an early Van der Graaf classic: musical passages of quiet beauty side by side with fierce sonic onslaughts, and a dramatic lyrical retelling of the major battle in the Song of Roland. Hammill's lyrics are a mixture of formal rigour and conversational tone. Comparing this song to 'Rift Valley', one can see how much Hammill's lyrical approach had changed in three years, and how little his subject matter had changed. Both songs deal speculatively with historical figures shrouded in varying degrees of myth. In the end, the high drama is undercut in a characteristically Van der Graafian fashion – as the music begins to fade out, jocular chatter, whooping, and coughing can be heard from the band members, reminding us that we're listening to Hammill listening to himself and the band playing a serious song but also embodying the lighter side of VdGG. A slightly wry chuckle would be hard to suppress, and wisely, some of his self-deprecating humour is baked into the final package.

'It All Went Red' (Evans, Hammill, Jackson)

Bits of the title track notwithstanding, this is the only recording to come from 1971. It was recorded during the *Pawn Hearts* sessions at the home of Charisma label boss Tony Stratton-Smith. Banton doesn't appear to be involved in this one; Hammill is credited with organ, and Evans and Jackson inhabit their usual roles.

Starting out as a relatively benign instrumental with only marginally sinister leanings, 'It All Went Red' quickly descends into nightmare territory, embodying the darker aspects of the 'Pawn Hearts' material. The organ and saxophone playing is deranged, and with Evans at the helm, the music careens like an amusement park car in a dark, interior haunted house ride. This is the band's *ALT* for 1971. It should be noted that, despite the printed tracklisting in later editions of *Time Vaults* on CD, this is the correct title, not 'It All Went Up'.

'Faint and Forsaken' (Hammill)

Time Vaults ends with two VdGG interpretations of solo Hammill songs. This one was recorded in the 1975 *Godbluff* sessions when Banton was actually present (unlike the above two tracks from the same period). As the title implies, this track is comprised of band performances of parts of two songs – 'Faint-Heart and the Sermon' and 'Forsaken Gardens', from the albums *In Camera* and *The Silent Corner and the Empty Stage*, respectively.

Since these songs were released in 1974, it seems likely that they were being rehearsed with an eye to playing them in a live setting – indeed, they were both staples of the reunion tour setlist. The track opens with a full-band performance of the instrumental break in the middle of 'Faint-Heart'. On the album track, Hammill played all the keyboard parts, but here, he, Banton, and Jackson each take one of the parts on their respective instruments – piano, organ, and saxophone – while Evans fleshes the piece out with drums, which were absent from the original version. The band version packs a bombastic punch that the *In Camera* layers of keyboards never quite attain.

The last minute of this short track features the instrumental middle section of 'Forsaken Gardens'. It's not terribly different from the album version, as the same musicians played the same instruments. But it does sound more like Van der Graaf, with a slightly more raucous feel to the playing.

'Black Room' (Hammill)

The previous track was a recording of parts of songs after the fact. On 'Black Room', we're treated to a band run-through of what would become, by default, a 'solo' song. Recorded in 1972, during the same sessions that produced 'Roncevaux', the band had intended for this to be on the next VdGG album, and, after the split, it ended up on Hammill's *Chameleon in the Shadow of the Night* 1973 LP. This is the one track on *Time Vaults* where Hammill's vocals are of the same vintage as the performance, instead of being recorded and dubbed in later.

The Live Albums

All of the albums discussed in this section were released after 2005, and, with two exceptions, are recordings of performances by the 21st Century four-piece or three-piece iterations of Van der Graaf Generator. They make up for a dearth of commercially available live recordings from the band's first decade.

Because VdGG existed in such short bursts of time in the 1970s, there never was enough time for the retrospective attention required to make a live album, and Peter Hammill, for one, was never interested in such a project. He was of the opinion that what transpired during a particular performance belonged to the performers and the audience, and wouldn't resonate with listeners who weren't experiencing it in the moment as it occurred. *Vital* came about partly because it was economically viable – it might have afforded the band a lifeline in the way of cash, and partly because that line-up of the band was so unique and powerful that its members, including Hammill, felt their live work should be documented. Due to the unique nature of *Vital*, with its wealth of previously unreleased songs, and startling rearrangements of existing tunes, I decided to put it with the 'regular' albums in chronological order in the book. In this section, we'll look at the remainder of the live VdGG catalogue.

Real Time (2007)

Personnel:
Hugh Banton: organ
Guy Evans: drums
Peter Hammill: vocals, guitar, piano
David Jackson: saxophone, flute
UK release date and label: March 2007; Fie!

When Van der Graaf Generator's reformation became public knowledge in 2005, making their 'comeback' album, *Present*, was only one of two hurdles facing the band, and probably the least daunting. They had also committed to playing live, for the first time in just under 30 years. Their first concert was to be at the Royal Festival Hall in London, on 6 May 2005, and it was a major event in the progressive rock and musical cognoscenti/hipster worlds. The possibility of going forward as a unit hung in the balance between the entering and exiting of that stage. The fact that you're reading this means, of course, that they pulled it off. The record of this fantastic, emotional, event, titled *Real Time*, was released almost two years later on Peter Hammill's own FIE! label, as a two-CD set.

By that time, of course, David Jackson had already left the band, but not before he was able to summon the ghost of VdGG past with his instantly recognisable flute call, prompting Hammill to whisper-sing the opening lines of 'The Undercover Man'. Van der Graaf returned to the stage with the majestic one-two punch that is the first side of their *Godbluff* album, which thus represent the first two tracks on the album. The remainder of *Real Time* follows the concert as it was performed, in, well, real time. The band included two songs from *Present* among the revisited 1970s classics, coming both from before and after the 1972-75 split. In the end, every VdGG album that the four members played on was represented, to varying extents. There was, understandably, nothing from *The Aerosol Grey Machine* or *The Quiet Zone / The Pleasure Dome*.

A 3CD edition of *Real Time* was released in Japan in 2007. The third CD contained live versions of 'Pilgrims', 'When She Comes', and 'Still Life', each from different concerts that occurred in Europe in July 2005, well after the show documented on the regular version of the album. In addition, there is a track titled 'Gibberish', which was pulled from the soundcheck of the same concert where 'When She Comes' was recorded.

Live at the Paradiso (2009)

Personnel:
Hugh Banton: organ
Guy Evans: drums
Peter Hammill: vocals, guitar, piano
UK release date and label: 2009; Voiceprint.

In 2007, VdGG, now a trio, began to tour again in advance of the *Trisector* album, due out the following year. The performance at the Paradiso in Amsterdam on 14 April, the tenth on this tour, was recorded (video and audio) and released in the UK in 2009 as both a 2 CD set and a DVD, each medium a separate release.

The setlist differs significantly from the four-piece VdGG shows of 2005. One of the show's centrepieces is a sneak preview of two new songs ('All That Before' and 'Lifetime). A few of the songs from the '70s remained from the 2005 concerts, but there were significant changes. Notably, 'A Place to Survive', in performance, was cut by more than half of its original length, and was rendered considerably tamer and more straightforward than its unruly predecessor. 'Every Bloody Emperor', from the first post-reformation album, was kept in the setlist, but 'Nutter Alert' was given a rest. From the solo Hammill material that overlapped into VdGG repertoire, '(In the) Black Room' remained, but, surprisingly, or perhaps not, 'Gog' was re-introduced and given the 21st Century treatment!

Recorded Live in Concert at Metropolis Studios, London (2012)

Personnel:
Hugh Banton: organ
Guy Evans: drums
Peter Hammill: vocals, guitar, piano
UK release date and label: June 2012; Salvo

Although the band toured heavily in 2008, the next recorded performance. In December 2010, Van der Graaf were invited to perform at Metropolis Studios before a very small, and closely-packed, audience. As before, the show was audio-visually recorded. In 2011, a DVD of the performance was released under the rather ambiguous title *Legends*. The following year, it was reissued in both audio and video formats, in a 2 CD / 1 DVD package, with the longer title. In 2014, it was released on vinyl as a 2 LP set.

Five years into their new lease on life as VdGG, the band had produced enough current material for the setlist to be weighed heavily in its favour. Out of 11 songs, only three were from the 1970s, and two of these comprised side one of *Pawn Hearts*. The other old song was 'Childlike Faith'. There were no songs performed from Hammill's solo catalogue. Although the new VdGG album was still months away from being released at the time of the concert, this live album wasn't available until much later in 2011, so it was only the small group in the audience that heard the three new songs from *A Grounding in Numbers*: 'Your Time Starts Now', 'Bunsho', and 'Mr. Sands'. Four songs were featured from *Trisector*, including 'Lifetime'. The others, all of which were regularly performed on the band's tour following that album, were 'Interference Patterns', 'Over the Hill', and '(We Are) Not Here'. From *Present*, 'Nutter Alert' was brought back into rotation, replacing 'Every Bloody Emperor'.

Merlin Atmos (2015)

Personnel:
Hugh Banton: organ
Guy Evans: drums
Peter Hammill: vocals, guitar, piano
Produced at The Organ Workshop and Sofa Sound, 2013-2014 by Hugh Banton and Peter Hammill
UK release date and label: February 2015; Esoteric.

Two years after *A Grounding in Numbers* was released, the band decided to tour again. For these performances, the band decided to do something that was radical, even for Van der Graaf. They decided to centre the upcoming concerts around one long, album side-length piece, and it was going to be 'Flight', from Peter Hammill's 1980 solo album, *A Black Box*.

The original version, due mainly to budgetary restrictions, was performed almost entirely by Hammill, who played piano, guitar, drums, and bass. The only additional musician on 'Flight' was David Jackson, who provided flute and saxophone accompaniment on a few sections. Thus, there weren't a lot of different instrumental parts that needed to be transferred to the current three-piece line-up, but even so; it was likely a formidable task. Guy Evans was in Hammill's early 1980s touring/recording band, the K Group, and had performed 'Flight' with him numerous times in concert; as he says in the

Merlin Atmos liner notes, 'Peter and I had embedded muscle memory of performing 'Flight' live'. Banton had never played it, however. Difficulties overcome, they pulled it off to much acclaim on the USA leg of their tour.

Reacting to the positive feedback from audiences, the band decided to keep going in the long-form direction. They worked on rehearsing 'A Plague of Lighthouse-Keepers', and added it to the repertoire for the second leg of their 2013 tour, in Europe. Thus, European audiences got to hear both 20-plus minute suites as well as a shorter than usual list of other favourites.

The Esoteric label released a collection of recordings from the 2013 European tour, titled *Merlin Atmos*. Esoteric seemed to have a knack for releasing multiple versions of their albums in different formats, and *Merlin Atmos* was no exception. There was a 2 CD set that contained both long pieces on the first disc, bookending some shorter songs, and a second CD, subtitled 'Bonus Atmos', containing more songs from various concerts on the European tour. There was also a single CD edition of the album, corresponding exactly to the first disc in the larger package. Going even more minimalist, a vinyl version was also released, containing only 'Flight' and 'A Plague of Lighthouse-Keepers', one per side. The task of mixing the material on the first CD fell to Banton, who did it at his home studio, while Hammill worked on the 'Bonus Atmos' disc, taking credit for 'assembling and balancing' the recordings.

Why the title? Hammill explained it in a newsletter: 'Merlin' was the brand name of an engine that powered many aircraft in the UK post-World War II, and it was the sound that Banton 'simulated' on his organ at the start and finish of 'Flight'. 'Atmos' was a word the band used to use to refer to the vibe in the crowd; short for 'atmosphere'.

After the Flood – At the BBC 1968-1977 (2015)

Personnel:
Hugh Banton: organ, piano, bass
Charles Dickie: cello, keyboards
Keith Ellis: bass
Guy Evans: drums
Peter Hammill: vocals, guitar, piano
David Jackson: saxophone, flute
Nic Potter: bass
Graham Smith: violin
UK release date and label: April 2015; Virgin
Running time: 2:34:56

Enter the BBC. Van der Graaf Generator recorded a number of 'live in studio' sessions for the BBC during the late 1960s and 1970s. A few of these were lost or of insufficient quality for commercial release, but there were some excellent VdGG performances captured on tape by the BBC. Four sessions were released in 1994 on a compilation CD titled *Maida Vale*, and other sessions appeared on the VdGG box set retrospective in 2000. All of these sessions, and more, were finally compiled and released in 2015 on a 2 CD set titled *After the Flood*. The earliest iterations of VdGG are the most heavily documented here. The first three tracks on disc one are from 1968, well before David Jackson and Nic Potter joined the group. The quartet of Banton, Evans, Hammill, and Keith Ellis performed 'People You Were Going To', 'Afterwards', and 'Necromancer' for a broadcast date of 18 November 1968. Nine more tracks were recorded in 1970 and 1971 over three sessions; one with the *Least We Can Do Is Wave*-era quintet, and the other two with the 'classic' four-piece line-up. Of particular interest is a rendition of 'Vision' with just Banton on piano and Hammill on vocals; as accomplished as the performance on *Fool's Mate* may be, this is arguably the definitive version. It's also interesting to hear 'Darkness' performed twice, once in 1970 with the quintet featuring Nic Potter on bass, and once in 1971 after Potter left and Banton took over bass duties.

Disc 2 of *After the Flood* focuses almost exclusively on the 1975-1977 era. Following the first track (a 1971 performance of 'Refugees' that likely happened alongside the Christmas hi-jinks detailed under *Time Vaults*), there are three sets of two songs each, from *Godbluff* (3 July 1975), *Still Life* (1 January 1976), and *World Record* (11 November 1976). The last three tracks are from the Van der Graaf (hold the Generator) line-up, and were broadcast on 24 October 1977: 'Cat's Eye', 'The Sphinx in the Face', and a version of the 'Plague of Lighthouse-Keepers / Sleepwalkers' medley that later turned up on *Vital*. These final tracks feature Charles Dickie on cello; he joined after *The Quiet Zone / The Pleasure Dome* was complete, so outside of the *Vital* album and the bonus tracks on the 2005 *Quiet Zone* reissue, this is the only place he can be heard with Van der Graaf.

Godbluff Live (2017)

Personnel:
Hugh Banton: organ
Guy Evans: drums
Peter Hammill: vocals, guitar, piano
David Jackson: saxophone, flute
Japan release date and label: March 2017: The Store for Music
Running time: 1:05:30

For many years, two legendary Van der Graaf Generator performances could only be viewed via bootlegged videocassette, usually so many generations from the source tape that it would be virtually unwatchable. These two performances included a 1971 Belgian television studio recording of 'Theme One' and 'A Plague of Lighthouse-Keepers' and a 1975 performance of the *Godbluff* album in its entirety. Both recordings were finally given a legitimate release in 2003, as *Godbluff Live 1975*. This title went in and out of print and was subsequently re-released numerous times, changing names and companies, and eventually adding on performances of 'Whatever Would Robert Have Said' and 'Darkness' from a German television broadcast in 1970. In 2017, a Japanese company released a high-quality audio-only version of the 1971 and 1975 performances.

It's worth noting that 'A Plague of Lighthouse-Keepers was never fully performed in one take until the 2013 tour. Although the 1971 video contains 'Plague' in its entirety, it was not performed in one consecutive take. Rather, the various parts of the suite were recorded throughout the length of a day; the band would have to stop and make adjustments, and editing sleight-of-hand was used to give an impression of continuity. Trickery aside, it's a fantastic performance, as is 'Theme One'. The *Godbluff* performance is also quite good from a technical standpoint, but not quite as rousing as the 1971 portion.

Live at Rockpalast – Leverkusen 2005 (2018)

Personnel:
Hugh Banton: organ
Guy Evans: drums
Peter Hammill: vocals, guitar, piano
David Jackson: saxophone, flute
UK release date and label: May 2018; MIG
Running time: 1:03:59

With the most recent addition to the live VdGG canon, we come full circle. The *Live at Rockpalast – Leverkusen 2005* 2 CD / DVD set was released in 2018. The first show of their reunion tour was captured on the *Real Time* album, and what was originally intended to be the climax of the 2005 tour was also recorded – but not released until 13 years later.

The band viewed the concert with a mix of confidence and mild anxiety; they had built their stage confidence back up through the course of the tour, but at the same time had taken a number of weeks off before this performance, so in that sense, were starting from zero again. To make things more interesting, it was not just an isolated VdGG concert, but a jazz festival appearance, which gave Evans, at least, some pause. As he put it in a quote in the album's liner notes: 'It was a little bit daunting to perform where so many legends had appeared, but the experience soon reminded me that the spirit of jazz is emotion and exploration, irrespective of definitions'. The occasion marked Peter Hammill's 57th birthday, and one of David Jackson's final performances with Van der Graaf Generator. Such were the highs and lows that characterised Van der Graaf Generator's brilliant live shows, and equally brilliant career.

On Track series

Queen – Andrew Wild 978-1-78952-003-3
Emerson Lake and Palmer – Mike Goode 978-1-78952-000-2
Deep Purple and Rainbow 1968-79 – Steve Pilkington 978-1-78952-002-6
Yes – Stephen Lambe 978-1-78952-001-9
Blue Oyster Cult – Jacob Holm-Lupo 978-1-78952-007-1
The Beatles – Andrew Wild 978-1-78952-009-5
Roy Wood and the Move – James R Turner 978-1-78952-008-8
Genesis – Stuart MacFarlane 978-1-78952-005-7
Jethro Tull – Jordan Blum 978-1-78952-016-3
The Rolling Stones 1963-80 – Steve Pilkington 978-1-78952-017-0
Judas Priest – John Tucker 978-1-78952-018-7
Toto – Jacob Holm-Lupo 978-1-78952-019-4
Van Der Graaf Generator – Dan Coffey 978-1-78952-031-6
Frank Zappa 1966 to 1979 – Eric Benac 978-1-78952-033-0
Elton John in the 1970s – Peter Kearns 978-1-78952-034-7
The Moody Blues – Geoffrey Feakes 978-1-78952-042-2
The Beatles Solo 1969-1980 – Andrew Wild 978-1-78952-030-9
Steely Dan – Jez Rowden 978-1-78952-043-9
Hawkwind – Duncan Harris 978-1-78952-052-1
Fairport Convention – Kevan Furbank 978-1-78952-051-4
Iron Maiden – Steve Pilkington 978-1-78952-061-3
Dream Theater – Jordan Blum 978-1-78952-050-7
10CC and Godley and Crème – Peter Kearns 978-1-78952-054-5
Gentle Giant – Gary Steel 978-1-78952-058-3
Kansas – Kevin Cummings 978-1-78952-057-6
Mike Oldfield – Ryan Yard 978-1-78952-060-6
The Who – Geoffrey Feakes 978-1-78952-076-7
Crosby, Stills and Nash – Andrew Wild 978-1-78952-039-2
U2 – Eoghan Lyng 978-1-78952-078-1
Barclay James Harvest – Keith and Monika Domone 978-1-78952-067-5
Steve Hackett – Geoffrey Feakes 978-1-78952-098-9
Renaissance – David Detmer 978-1-78952-062-0
Dire Straits – Andrew Wild 978-1-78952-044-6
Camel – Hamish Kuzminski 978-1-78952-040-8
Rush – Will Romano 978-1-78952-080-4
Joni Mitchell – Peter Kearns 978-1-78952-081-1
UFO – Richard James 978-1-78952-073-6
Kate Bush – Bill Thomas 978-1-78952-097-2
Asia – Pete Braidis 978-1-78952-099-6
Aimee Mann – Jez Rowden 978-1-78952-036-1
Pink Floyd Solo – Mike Goode 978-1-78952-046-0
Gong – Kevan Furbank 978-1-78952-082-8

Decades Series
Pink Floyd in the 1970s – Georg Purvis 978-1-78952-072-9
Marillion in the 1980s – Nathaniel Webb 978-1-78952-065-1
Focus in the 1970s – Stephen Lambe 978-1-78952-079-8
Curved Air in the 1970s – Laura Shenton 978-1-78952-069-9

On Screen series
Carry On... – Stephen Lambe 978-1-78952-004-0
Seinfeld Seasons 1 to 5 – Stephen Lambe 978-1-78952-012-5
Monty Python – Steve Pilkington 978-1-78952-047-7
Doctor Who: The David Tennant Years – Jamie Hailstone 978-1-78952-066-8
James Bond – Andrew Wild 978-1-78952-010-1
David Cronenberg – Patrick Chapman 978-1-78952- 071-2

Other Books
Maximum Darkness – Deke Leonard 978-1-78952-048-4
The Twang Dynasty – Deke Leonard 978-1-78952-049-1
Tommy Bolin: In and Out of Deep Purple – Laura Shenton 978-1-78952-070-5
Jon Anderson and the Warriors - the road to Yes – David Watkinson 978-1-78952-059-0
Derek Taylor: For Your Radioactive Children - Andrew Darlington 978-1-78952-038-5
20 Walks Around Tewkesbury – Stephen Lambe 978-1-78952-074-3

and many more to come!

Would you like to write for Sonicbond Publishing?

We are mainly a music publisher, but we also occasionally publish in other genres including film and television. At Sonicbond Publishing we are always on the look-out for authors, particularly for our two main series, On Track and Decades.

Mixing fact with in depth analysis, the On Track series examines the entire recorded work of a particular musical artist or group. All genres are considered from easy listening and jazz to 60s soul to 90s pop, via rock and metal.

The Decades series singles out a particular decade in an artist or group's history and focuses on that decade in more detail than may be allowed in the On Track series.

While professional writing experience would, of course, be an advantage, the most important qualification is to have real enthusiasm and knowledge of your subject. First-time authors are welcomed, but the ability to write well in English is essential.

Sonicbond Publishing has distribution throughout Europe and North America, and all our books are also published in E-book form. Authors will be paid a royalty based on sales of their book. Further details about our books are available from www.sonicbondpublishing.com. To contact us, complete the contact form there or email info@sonicbondpublishing.co.uk